# Irreparable Damage
# (Irreparable, #1)

## By
## Sam Mariano

Irreparable Damage (Irreparable, #1)

ISBN-13: 978-1503227491

ISBN-10: 1503227499

---

## DEDICATION:

TO MY READERS—YOU GUYS ARE SUPER AWESOME.

THANK YOU!

# CHAPTER ONE

Once her parents and younger brother went to bed, Willow Kensington was psyched to finally have the house to herself.

Her 18th birthday had just passed, and between the cake, cupcakes, and the "birthday ice cream" her boyfriend had taken her out for, she desperately needed to burn some calories before indulging in some late night television.

After changing into her work-out clothes, she briefly considered putting in an exercise video. Since it was unseasonably cool out for June, she opted to go for a run instead.

Putting on some upbeat music, she did a few basic warm-up exercises, rotated her ankles several times each way, and set off along her usual path in their little suburban neighborhood.

By the time she made it back home, Willow was beat. The front porch only had four steps, but her muscles burned as she took the last two. Tugging her ear buds out, she shoved them in the front pocket of her sweater, attempting to turn the doorknob, but found it locked. Weird. Her mom or Ashlynn must've gotten up for some reason and locked it, assuming she was upstairs in bed.

Reaching into the hanging planter, she felt around the soil until she retrieved the spare key, thankful that she didn't have to wake anyone up.

A half hour later, clean and wearing comfy clothes, Willow felt like a new person. She was still thirsty though, so she ran back downstairs to get a bottle of water.

As she stood bent over, peering into the refrigerator, the tiny hairs on the back of her neck stood on end; her body tensed and she had the oddest sensation that someone was staring at her.

Straightening slowly, she glanced to the left—half expecting to see her brother creeping up on her—but nothing was there.

Shoulders slumping in relief, she reached into the refrigerator, grabbed her water, and closed the door.

Two strong arms closed around her from behind. The water slipped out of her hands as the man anchored her arms against her body. She opened her mouth to scream and a third gloved hand came from off to the side, roughly covering her mouth.

"Hold her still," a male voice barked quietly.

"I'm trying, she's fucking squirming," the other one muttered, pulling her more roughly up against his body. "Christ, stop moving!"

Willow thrashed even more, her protests muffled as she continued to kick and yank her arms wildly, trying to break free, trying to call for help. Her heart slammed against her rib cage and she could scarcely draw a breath—either because she was panicking, or because the man's hand had most of her nose covered. A bit frantically, she wondered if she was going to suffocate—if they were *planning* to kill her? Would they leave her body in the kitchen floor for her family to find the next morning?

The one barking the orders yanked her arm straight, holding her forearm firmly enough to bruise it, and warned the other man again to hold her still.

Then she saw the needle poised above the veins in her arm.

She attempted to scream again, just as uselessly as before since her mouth was still covered. Her horror grew as the other man readied the needle.

"No," she cried, incoherently. She tried to beg, to plead, to bargain, but they couldn't make out anything she was trying to say. Tears welled up in her eyes as she kicked backward, managing to strike her captor in the shin several

● ● ●
*6*

times, but it only resulted in him cussing at her and squeezing her until she was afraid her ribs might crack.

The needle slid into her vein and she could only watch as he pushed whatever it contained into her body.

A sob tore from her throat as the one holding her shifted her weight, and she nearly got an arm free.

Willow tried once more to plead with them, but they had already injected her, so if it wasn't just to knock her out, it was too late anyway.

There was no time to think about it—no time to even consider that these terrifying moments might be her last. Suddenly every part of her body felt leaden, and everything went black.

# CHAPTER TWO

As the light flickered overhead, Ethan Wilde shifted in the uncomfortable plastic seat at the dingy Laundromat, missing the comfort of his home more than ever.

Leaving his family for extended periods was always hard, but leaving with a one-month-old son at home had been damn near impossible.

He didn't have a choice though. When his inside contact told him Delmonico's crew had a spot open for a smart, trustworthy guy, he threw Ethan's name into the hat.

Well, Jack's name. His fake name was Jack.

Now that he had four people at home depending on him, he should probably start thinking about getting out of that particular line of work. Or at least sticking to safer jobs.

While he waited for his clothes to dry, he sauntered over to the bathroom.

Once inside, he took the opportunity to check his email. He hadn't been able to check it for a while but he had a second phone on him in case he got a chance.

After 50 new emails loaded, he scrolled through, most of it inconsequential or irrelevant, given his current location. Only two emails marked urgent. He tapped the first one, a missing 14-year-old girl, Hispanic, there was a picture attached along with the last seen information, $5,000 reward. Couldn't look for her while he was neck-deep in his current operation, but he'd keep an eye out. The chances of running across her were pretty slim, but the girl in the picture looked older than she was, so even though none of the girls back at Delmonico's seemed 14, he could check it out.

The next urgent email was from the family of yet another missing girl, desperate to locate her and able to pay for extra eyes to look. That one was older, prettier—newly 18, light brown hair, gray eyes, 5'5" and 115 lbs, $10,000 reward on that one. He took a look at her photo, just on the off chance he stumbled across her, but that one he expected even less. Back at Delmonico's, there were exactly zero beautiful white American girls. Too risky.

He didn't want to risk responding, so instead he closed his email and ripped the SIM card out of his phone, tearing off a piece of paper towel and wrapping it up, then dropping it into the toilet and flushing.

His other phone went off—the one he pretended was his real phone with Delmonico's crew. It was Tito telling him to pick up a case of beer.

Rolling his eyes, Ethan made his way out of the bathroom and over to check on his laundry. The machine had stopped and everything had dried, so he shoved all the clothes into the laundry basket. Everything would be wrinkled as hell, but it didn't matter.

Outside, he threw his basket of rapidly wrinkling clothes into the backseat of his beat up Toyota, slid behind the wheel, and headed to the store to pick up some alcohol.

---

Turning the key in the ignition, Ethan heaved a sigh, trying to get his head back in the game. He probably shouldn't have checked his email. While he was living amongst the rats, it was easiest to pretend he was one of them until he believed it himself. Reminders of his real life made it harder to stomach the guys he was about to spend his evening with.

The street, sparsely lined with trees, was packed full of little rectangular homes, many converted into apartments or duplexes, stacked one on top of the other. Given that two people couldn't walk side-by-side between the houses, there wasn't a lot of perceived privacy, so it wasn't the kind of place you would expect criminals to imprison up to a dozen young women.

But that's what they did.

The house on the left contained a normal family—balding dad with glasses, seriously pregnant mom, and a little blonde girl with a My Little Pony backpack. They never so much as looked toward the house, even when Ethan was coming or going during the day and they were outside.

To the right was a brick building that Delmonico owned and rented out to four heroin addicts. Not the greatest of tenants, but they also weren't going to report any suspicious goings-on, even if by some miracle they noticed any.

They were hiding in plain sight.

So was he, so he couldn't exactly criticize their technique.

Upon entering the house, he made a conscious effort to adopt a much douchier demeanor. Glancing in the living room as he stepped into the grungy kitchen, he saw Chuck sprawled in the corner of the couch, but nobody else. There was no way anybody left Chuck there by himself, so Tito must be around somewhere.

Shoving the case into the barren refrigerator, Ethan grabbed one of the cold stragglers from the last case, popping it open and making his way to the cheap, old floral-print couch.

"So, did I miss anything good today?" he asked, plopping onto the opposite corner and tipping his beer back.

"Kinda," Chuck responded, but he didn't expand on that.

"Did Lane figure out when we're moving the first bunch yet?"

"Nah, not yet. Max is still beatin' around the fuckin' bush. Why, you got a hot date or something?"

Scoffing, Ethan said, "I wish, the only action I'm seeing lately is Tito kissing Lane's ass."

The other man grinned. "I know that's right."

They made inane small talk for a while. Chuck was one of the dumber criminals Ethan had come across, and it seemed like dumb luck that he wasn't in jail. Lane, the leader of that particular crew, knew that, so it wasn't surprising that Chuck didn't know anything. Most likely they would wait until the last minute to give specific dates and times. He wished they would hurry so he could pass along the intel and get the hell out of there.

The group of girls they were moving to Max's included a 15-year-old Mexican girl named Lorena—the girl he was there for. Some teens looked older than they were, but not Lorena—she looked younger. The few times he saw her, it had been difficult to stay in character. Every time she appeared, her face was a mask of terror. He didn't even want to think about what was happening to her behind the closed door of the room the girls were stashed in. It turned his stomach just to walk by that room, so he made a point to stay out of it.

Some of the guys made a point to go *into* it, but he tried not to think about that.

He wished it surprised him, but he had a pretty clear picture of how shitty people could be.

Just a few more days and they could all go home.

Tito emerged from one of the house's three bedrooms—the one the guys slept in, not the girls. That was a relief. He looked uncharacteristically tense though—Tito was usually a pretty chill guy.

"Everything okay?" Ethan asked, catching Tito's eye.

Nodding jerkily, Tito said, "Yeah, I guess."

"I brought the beer."

"Good man," Tito replied, making his way into the kitchen.

"It's not cold," Ethan told him.

"I don't give a fuck."

Shrugging, Ethan turned his gaze toward the tv, which Chuck was laughing at. "We on our own tonight?"

He hoped so. Tito and Chuck weren't so bad to kill a few hours with, but Ethan did not like Lane one bit. Some people, like Tito and Chuck, were in that line of business because they didn't think they had any better prospects and they needed the money. Lane was in it for the power. For the ability to hurt people and be praised for it.

Lane was an asshole.

And probably a sociopath, if Ethan had to guess.

Heading back into the living room, Tito planted his skinny ass in the mismatched recliner by the couch. "Naw. Lane's around."

Of course he was.

Ethan merely nodded, focusing his attention back on the tv.

The door to the room full of girls swung open and out stepped Lane. As soon as Lane saw Ethan sitting on the couch, he halted. "You're back."

Lifting his eyebrows and smirking casually, Ethan said, "Didn't realize I'd be missed. Had to do some laundry."

"Jack brought beer," Chuck announced.

Lane smiled thinly, nodded at Tito, then turned and walked back into the room.

Tito got up, setting his beer down on the coffee table, and headed back there with Lane.

A moment later Lane reappeared without Tito, but that time his entrance was much noisier and he wasn't alone.

Stumbling to keep pace with him as he dragged her by the arm was one of the girls—not one he had seen before. The girl was pale with wavy brown hair down past her bare breasts. She wore a scanty black skirt, a blindfold, and rope bound her hands together at the wrists.

The girls were rarely brought out of the room by themselves, and when they were, it wasn't good news. Lane usually seemed to prefer one of the other girls, but maybe he had a new favorite. Ethan felt a passing wave of sympathy for her—he couldn't imagine the bastard would be gentle.

"Well, don't be rude," Lane said lightly. "Come say hi."

Ethan rose to his feet, glancing at the girl. "She new?"

"Brand new. What do you think?"

Forcing a casual nod, he said simply, "Nice."

Lane nodded his agreement. "She's all yours. We saved her for you."

Brow furrowing in confusion, Ethan said, "Uh, whaddya mean?"

Catching on faster than Ethan, Chuck offered an enthusiastic, "Nice!"

"She was acting up earlier," Lane supplied. "She needs to be broken in a bit."

"I don't," the girl cried. "I—I told you, I…I'm sorry."

"Sorry only counts the first time," Lane stated. "After the first sorry, you tried to kick me in the testicles."

"I was afraid," she objected, her voice rising.

Lane's jaw clenched and his hand on her arm must have tightened, because she couldn't see, but the girl shrunk away from him.

Good survival instincts. Lane didn't seem like someone you should yell at.

The way she flinched though, he guessed Lane probably hit her in their earlier scuffle. Not that he should be surprised that Lane would hit a woman. Not that Lane thought of the girls as *people*.

Christ.

Before Lane could react, Ethan cut in, "Seems like she figured out her place."

Making a non-committal noise, he replied, "Still. Have a go."

Chuckling uneasily, Ethan said, "I don't know."

Chuck chose then to chime in. "Aw, c'mon, you were just sayin' you needed to get you some pussy."

"Yeah, but this… isn't what I meant," he said, forcing a half-ass smile. "You don't buy a bitch dinner first, you don't feel like you earned it, y'know."

Chuck uttered a bark of laughter. "Dinner—look here, Jackie's a gentleman."

Lane wasn't amused. Frowning in Ethan's direction, he said, "Don't tell me you've got a weak stomach. It's one of the few perks of the job. Everyone else has taken a turn—

you're the only one who hasn't tried out any of the girls. What's that about?"

Typically Ethan kept cool under pressure. With Lane looking at him for the first time with something akin to suspicion, he got a little hot under the collar.

"C'mon, don't be a pussy," Chuck said, approaching the terrified girl. He reached out and pinched one of her tits, causing the already trembling girl to flinch and a muffled sob escaped. "Look at these, don't tell me you don't want to hold onto these while you're fucking her. She's a lot better looking than the one I fucked. Hell, if you don't want her, I'll bite the bullet and break this one in."

"You're a real martyr," Lane said dryly. "No, this one's for Jack."

Stifling a sigh of frustration, Ethan forced a casual smile and a nod. "Alright, alright, you talked me into it. Which room's empty?"

Chuck started to point in the direction of the empty room but Lane interrupted, raising a single hand. "No room. Break her in right here."

Ethan stared at the other man. "Right here? In front of you guys?"

"Is that a problem?" Lane asked coolly.

"Hell yeah, it's a fucking problem," Ethan said, making a face. "Man, I can't get hard with you and Chuck watching. That's some voyeuristic bullshit right there."

Lane glanced over at Chuck, but Chuck was as dumb as a bag of socks and didn't smell anything fishy.

Ethan was starting to get really fucking nervous. It was all he could do to keep from checking to see if Lane had his pistol tucked into his pants. *That* would be even more suspicious.

He needed to stay cool. He needed to stay fucking cool. Yeah, he wanted to go home—but not in a body bag. Images of his beautiful raven-haired wife, their daughter and two sons flashed before his eyes.

Peering at the girl, he also knew intellectually that *someone* would "break her in." Chuck was salivating at the chance. Lane… Ethan suspected Lane was a sadist, so she definitely wouldn't want Lane to touch her.

Not that she wanted any of them to touch her.

Tito came strolling in from the back room where the rest of the girls were kept. "I could get used to having all these girls around." Then, noticing the tension in the room, he asked, "What's wrong?"

Lane spoke first. "Jack here seems to be prudish about where he fucks." Glancing at Jack, he smiled thinly and said,

"You *were* going to fuck her in the back room, weren't you? The empty one?"

"Of course," Ethan said, and instantly flinched, hearing the defensiveness in his own tone.

Fuck, fuck, fuck. He was fucking everything up. Tito caught his eye, and he was staring daggers—since Tito vouched for him, if they thought something was up with Jack/Ethan, they would blame Tito.

The mental body count was getting a little nerve-racking.

He attempted to manufacture an excuse they could believe.

"I just… honestly, you can bust my balls all you want, but I don't think I can get it up with you guys watching. I'm not into that shit."

"Let's see," Lane replied, walking over to the girl and removing her blindfold. When it looked like she might protest again, he grabbed her roughly by the jaw, jerking her gaze to his. "If you open your fucking mouth again, I'm going to give you something decidedly less pleasant than a gag to occupy it, are we clear?"

The girl's gray eyes widened in terror and she nodded jerkily.

Hit with recognition, Ethan felt like someone socked him in the stomach. The girl they wanted him to rape was the same 18-year-old missing person he had been emailed about hours earlier.

"No one's had a turn with her yet?"

Lane shook his head. "All yours, Jackie-boy."

Although she still appeared to be frightened, the girl raised her gaze to meet his and briefly appraised him. He knew what she was seeing—tall, lean, pitch black hair, ice blue eyes, dark stubble along his strong jaw since he hadn't had a chance to shave in a couple of days. Ethan knew he was attractive, especially when the only other guys in the room were Tito, Lane and Chuck.

But attractive didn't make rape go down any easier.

Just thinking about it made him sick to his stomach. There was no way in hell he'd be able to perform. Sure, he'd be mocked mercilessly, but at least he would have a valid excuse. Then he'd take the girl into a private room where he wouldn't be so "shy" and he'd pretend to have sex with her. It would get the guys off his back and hopefully save her from being raped by one of them.

It was the best plan he could come up with under the circumstances.

They needed to transport the fucking girls so he could get the one he came for and get the fuck out of their shitty-ass thug life.

Never, ever again. He was never going undercover so deep ever, ever again. Once he got himself out of there alive, it would be cheating spouses, fraudulent injury claims, and finding girls who hadn't been abducted by crime rings. Nothing more strenuous than that.

Ethan wished he could let her in on his plan without signaling everyone else, but he couldn't, so as he shook his head and unzipped his jeans, the horror in her eyes grew. The look of accusation she leveled at him went straight to his gut, but that was good—made it even more unlikely he would be able to rise to the occasion.

As expected, he was not aroused. When he moved to stand behind the girl and lifted up the tiny skirt they had put on her (nothing underneath) he tried not to look right at her round, firm ass as moved his hand over it, giving it a light smack that made the girl jump.

He had to make it seem like he was really trying.

"Is that one Antonio's daughter?" Tito suddenly asked.

Lane merely nodded, that thin smile spreading across his face again.

"Wouldn't we make more money off this bitch if we just ransomed her to her daddy?" Tito pointed out, probably trying to think of a way to save Ethan.

"Fuck Antonio. We'll get our money—out of the bitch's pussy," Lane stated.

If they were talking about the Antonio he thought they were talking about, he suddenly wanted to fuck the girl even less. Even if he made it out of the little leagues unscathed, her father would probably track him down and burn his house to the ground with Ethan and his whole family still inside.

A bead of sweat trickled down his forehead. What the fuck had he gotten himself into? Amanda had been telling him ever since Alison was born that he needed to stop taking dangerous cases, that one day he would get himself into a mess he couldn't get out of.

Of all the things for her to be right about.

"He has a point," Ethan chimed in. "Antonio's her dad? Antonio Castellanos? You would make a lot more if you ransomed her. I also… don't want to be castrated when he finds out I raped his daughter."

"They're not close," Lane said, as if that made all the difference. "She was illegitimate, a fling—not a daughter he actually raised. Still, he'll be insulted when he finds out she's making Delmonico money on her back."

Ethan knew Delmonico didn't like Castellanos, but that seemed like a truly terrible idea—especially for him.

That time, the girl spoke up. "He'll pay a ransom. We aren't that close but he'll pay a ransom as long as I'm unharmed."

"What did I say about speaking?" Lane snapped.

Ethan couldn't see her face since he was behind her, so he had to look to Lane to see if he seemed satisfied. He did, so she must have submitted.

"Get on with it," Lane said, throwing his arms into the air. "I don't have all day to sit around waiting for you to get hard."

"It's not happening," Ethan said, making a show of trying again to get himself going. "I'm telling you, I can't perform with an audience."

"Please," the girl said, her face tilted up toward Lane.

The least sympathetic person in the room, Lane's eyes flashed to the girl's face, cool fury gracing his features. "What *did* I say about that mouth of yours?" Then, taking a step toward the girl, he took her jaw roughly in his hand. "I think I have a solution to your little problem, Jackie. And it solves my obedience problem as well. Girl, turn and face Jack."

Well, that made him nervous. The girl unsteadily turned around, cautiously glancing up at him through the curtain of coppery brown hair that fell in her face.

"It'll be your job to get Jackie here up to the occasion. I warned you about that mouth, but you can't seem to keep it shut, so we might as well put it to good use."

Oh God, he couldn't mean… Ethan shook his head before he could stop himself. "No way, she'll bite it off."

"No, she won't," Lane said calmly, extracting the gun Ethan had been wondering about from his waistband and pointing it at the girl's temple. She whimpered, her face crumpling, and Ethan felt like a monster, even though none of it was his fault.

"On your knees," Lane directed.

The girl dropped to her knees, tears glistening in her eyes.

Ethan struggled to keep it together. He couldn't do it. He couldn't. More aware of how trapped he was than ever before, he glanced around the room, pondering what kind of chance he had of making it out alive if he grabbed the girl and started shooting. Assuming Lane didn't shoot him first, since he already had his gun at the ready.

Not good chances.

Even if he did, he'd be marked a traitor and they'd come looking for him. The way he intended to exit, no one would ever know Jack didn't actually exist.

He couldn't put his family in potential danger, and he wasn't ready to die.

Consequently, even though he hated himself, when she leaned in, reluctantly anchoring one hand on his hip, he watched her take his flaccid cock in her soft hand and start rubbing. When the traitorous little bastard sprang to life, he tilted his head back and groaned as she licked her lips and slowly closed her mouth over the length of him.

Just like that, his valid excuse evaporated.

Even trying to think about the onlookers didn't make him go limp. The girl's mouth and tongue were on the opposing team, and they were much more persuasive.

"All right," Lane said sharply. "You don't want to finish him off."

The girl pulled back, her pale face wet, red splotches all over each cheek.

That helped a little, but he still had a fucking hard-on.

With one more thin smile, Lane told Ethan to get to it, and even though a piece of his soul died as he did, Ethan had no choice; he helped the girl up and turned her around—he didn't want to look at her face while he did it—bent her over, and spread her feminine lips with his thumbs, easing the tip of his cock inside before stopping.

"Wait, I need a condom. I don't have a condom."

Ever helpful, Chuck pulled one out of his wallet and tossed it at him.

Swallowing back the bile that rose as the girl in front of him began to sob, Ethan withdrew the tip and slid the condom down over his penis.

Why couldn't it just deflate? He should have tried harder to get into the oral so he could've finished in her mouth instead.

"Oh, *fuck*," he practically hissed as he gradually pushed himself inside of her unwilling body. Holy fuck, was she tight. Grabbing her by the hips for leverage, he slowly pulled back out and then thrust forward with more force.

The girl cried out in pain, then sobbed even harder.

His cock softened a little at the sound. He rubbed his hand over her ass again, then moved his hand between her legs, wishing she was even the slightest bit wet to ease his passage. Since she wasn't, he located her clit and stimulated the little bundle of nerves. Her body shuddered and he heard her gasp, so he kept rubbing it, for a split second enjoying the sound of her helpless little moans, then he caught himself, remembering the circumstances and feeling like a sack of shit.

"This isn't for *her*," Lane reminded him. "Don't spoil the bitch."

*Fucker*. But Ethan stopped, not wanting to piss Lane off, repositioning one hand on her ass and the other on her hip.

As soon as he began thrusting inside of her again, her crying picked back up. It was already done at that point, so he allowed himself a few peeks at her to keep up his stimulation, figuring it best for both of them if he powered through it as quickly as possible.

When he came, for a split second he was able to forget everything else, and have one last moment of peace.

Then he pulled out of her and she crumpled to her knees, hugging herself as she crouched in the floor, still crying.

Then he looked down at the condom, and it got a million times worse. There was blood on the condom. Quite a bit of blood. Glancing at the girl, he saw a streak of blood smeared on the inside of her thigh.

He knew he had to have hurt her, but as he reviewed the blood and the moment when she had cried out sharply....

His heart plummeted; his blood froze in his veins.

"Were you a virgin?" he asked without thought, and without containing his horror.

It was barely perceptible, but the tiny nodding movement her head made broke even more of his soul.

"Jesus Christ," he muttered to himself, bringing his hand to his eyes and tiredly passing his hand up over his forehead. "Jesus Christ, Lane. You gave me a fucking virgin?"

"How was I supposed to know?" Lane asked, without remorse. "I didn't ask. As old as she is, I assumed she wasn't."

Looking down at the girl, Ethan so badly wanted to apologize. It wouldn't fix anything, of course, he had already wronged her in a way he could never right, and that knowledge would eat away at him for the rest of his life.

But he wished there was someone to console her in that moment, even if it was him.

No one would. He couldn't.

His stomach pitched and for a split second, he thought he was going to be sick.

He managed to keep from vomiting, but the roiling in his stomach was unpleasant and persistent. Guilt, newly blossomed, already began to eat away at him, and he hadn't even taken the fucking condom off yet.

If they didn't get out of there soon, he wasn't sure he would have a life to go back to.

# Chapter Three

They finally nailed down the details.

In the two days leading up to the big one, Ethan had kept close watch on the gray-eyed girl—and more importantly, any of the guys who looked in her direction.

He still felt like a huge sack of shit, but he had already determined if another guy tried to rape her, he would do whatever he could to stop it. Short of gunfire, because he had mulled it over again and any way he looked at it, that was a bad option. He could feign being territorial over her—or, really, not even feign it. Since he wanted to ensure that she made it to safety at least without being gang raped, he *would* be territorial over her if it helped her.

Chuck went sniffing around her the previous night, but Ethan leveled a contentious glare in his direction. Chuck held his hands up in mock surrender and walked off smirking.

Since the rape, being around the guys who watched him do it made him ill. Before that, he had been able to stomach them by getting lost in the character he was playing, but actually harming someone… that had prematurely strangled his ability to pretend he was someone else.

Nope, he was Ethan Wilde, married father of three. He had a little girl—just like the girl he raped was someone's little girl.

It made him absolutely sick.

He didn't know how he was ever going to look his daughter in the eye again.

Virgin or not it was unforgivable, of course, but knowing that for whatever reason, she had chosen not to have sex with *anyone* up to that point—and knowing based on her looks it couldn't be from lack of opportunity—seemed to amplify his sins. How was she going to cope with what happened to her? How would any of them? The other ones he had only been unable to help, but the one with the gray eyes…he damaged her himself, and he would probably be seeing her in his nightmares for the rest of his life.

She would probably be seeing *him* in hers.

It wasn't until the day following the rape that he realized saving her would mean ruining himself.

If everything went as planned and they got out, the police would take her statement about what ills she had suffered while in captivity.

He was going to be arrested. For real.

And then, if Antonio was her father and he liked her enough to be protective, he was going to have a very bad time in the system. Hell, he might never make it out, and even if he did, Amanda would be gone, the kids would have grown up without him.

The full gravity of the situation was suddenly hitting him, and it was not a pretty picture. He couldn't *look* at the girl without thinking about how saving her would ruin his life. For a split second, he reconsidered, but then his soul felt even blacker, and of course he couldn't *actually* leave her in hell to save his own ass.

Maybe he could talk to her before the police did, beg her not to—

No, he couldn't do that either. He wanted to, but he had done enough damage, and asking her to protect her attacker was something he couldn't bring himself to do.

All he could do at that point was hope for the best, even though he wasn't sure what the best case scenario even was anymore. That Amanda would understand? That he might get a light sentencing since he *had* retrieved two missing girls and cooperated with the police? Antonio not wanting his balls in a vice?

None of the best case scenarios seemed like much to look forward to.

---

Max's place was technically a pizza parlor, but he ran an illicit prostitution ring out of the back rooms. Up until that point, he'd used local women who "worked" there, but the women he had were getting old and tired, and he needed some younger girls to lure in the clientele.

The girls in question were loaded into a pewter colored Astro van with tinted windows and shuttled to Max's place. Three of the girls were silent the whole time, per Lane's barked orders—the one he was originally there to extract sobbing quietly, afraid of what was going to happen to her next. The one with the gray eyes didn't cry, she merely stared straight ahead until she finally asked, "Where are you taking us?"

Nobody answered her, and when Ethan glanced at her she promptly put her head down.

They pulled up behind the back door to unload the girls. Ethan and Chuck were charged with taking the girls inside, while Tito stood guard outside the back door. Since there were four girls and two guys, Ethan wanted to make sure he had the two girls he needed to extract close by, so he took each girl by the wrist, leaving Chuck with the other two. The gray-eyed girl flinched when he grabbed her, while the other merely glanced at him, unfazed.

Now that it was getting down to go-time, he would typically feel sharper, more focused, but because of everything that happened, he was distracted, off his game, and that made him nervous. He wasn't doing anyone any favors if he fucked up in the final lap.

After escorting the girls into the back room, Ethan volunteered to stay and keep an eye on them while Chuck went to verify that the girls were in their room.

It wasn't much of a room. A tiny area with block walls, no window, a unit of beat up metal lockers in the back corner, an end table with a tall lamp beside it, and three cots squeezed in there corner to corner. Honestly he didn't even know how they managed to cram it all in there. He also didn't understand why three cots for four girls. The ground was cold cement, so it wasn't exactly a good place for the girls to sleep.

Not that Max cared about their comfort, obviously.

He guessed it might have been a break room at one time, but even for a break room it was small.

Turning to glance at the girls, he saw that the gray-eyed one had seated herself on the cot farthest away from him. Lorena sat with a short-haired girl on one of the beds closest to him and the exit, while the girl who spoke no English sat on his other side.

Pointing to the gray-eyed girl and then the one who didn't speak English, he told them to switch beds, first in English, then in Spanish. The gray-eyed girl didn't move.

"I'm fine here," she stated.

Sighing, he said, "I need you over here."

"Why?"

"Just in case."

"Just in case what?"

It was like arguing with his four-year-old.

"Just switch fucking cots," he said impatiently, then he took a step outside the door to check in each direction.

When he turned around, the gray-eyed one still hadn't moved, but the non-English-speaking girl was perched next to her on the bed, looking at him cautiously.

Ethan shook his head, but since he couldn't risk blowing his cover, he didn't repeat himself.

A couple minutes passed and then Chuck came down the hall and ducked into the room. "Having fun back here?"

"Loads," Ethan said dryly.

"We're 'bout to get out of here so say your goodbyes. Hey, look on the bright side—at least you know where she is if you wanna pay her a visit."

It was a stupid, insensitive joke, but Chuck was a stupid, insensitive guy so Ethan wasn't surprised.

• • •
*34*

Shifting his weight, Ethan glanced behind him at the girls, four faces, all of them shadowed by fear.

Just as he was about to make his way out of the room, Tito came running down the hall, panic all across his features. "We gotta go!"

"What's wrong?" Chuck asked with a frown.

"Five unmarked cars—get the fuck out!"

That was the last thing Tito said before turning around and booking back out of the place himself.

Chuck cursed and went off in the other direction, then turned around uncertainly toward the exit. He must have been more afraid of Lane than the cops, because he went the other way to warn them.

Okay, the shit was hitting the fan. Turning around, in a tone that brooked absolutely no argument, Ethan shot the stubborn girl a hard look. "Get over here now!"

She tensed, but she didn't get up.

"Now!"

She jumped up, her gaze darting toward the door, but she finally listened and got on the cot behind him. While she did, he turned to his other charge and told her to get on the same cot, and that one moved without question.

"What's going on?" Gray Eyes asked.

"The cops are busting us. Stay behind me," he said, pulling his own gun out, checking it to make sure he was ready in case he needed to use it.

"If the cops are here, you're already busted," she said desperately. "Let us go!"

"I'm not holding you prisoner, I'm keeping you safe. If it ends in gunfire, guess who isn't armed?" he shot back.

"Says the bad guy holding the gun," she fired right back. "If that's illegal, you're going to get additional charges."

He spared her a look of disbelief. "Are you really lecturing me on the law right now?"

She shrugged, stretching her neck toward the door. "Just saying."

"Listen," he said lowly. "I know you hate me, and you have every right to hate me, but for the love of God, if I tell you to stay or run or anything else, I need you to listen to me, okay?"

"Yeah, okay," she said sarcastically.

"I mean it," he said. Looking back one more time, he said, "I have a wife and three kids at home, so I'd like to survive tonight and not get shot at trying to save your ass."

Her eyes widened and she didn't respond immediately, so he turned his attention back to the door, peering out into the hall one more time. No one was running down it, so that could be a good sign.

When he pulled back, he heard the girl mutter, "I guess even bad guys have families."

"Yeah, well, I'd like to return you safely to yours, so just…listen to me for 10 minutes, okay?"

"Return me to my family?" she demanded, the disbelief evident in her tone. "Please, I'm not a fucking moron."

Even though he knew it shouldn't give him any satisfaction, he glanced back. "Lauren Kensington and Ashlynn Sanders?"

The girl's face froze. "How do you know those names?"

Ethan sighed. "I'm a private investigator, this is what I do for a living. Now please… stop distracting me right now."

Instead of complying, she demanded more answers. "You're what? This is your fucking process, are you kidding me?"

"I had to blend in, if they knew I was lying to them, they wouldn't have thought twice about killing me. I can't explain this to you right now, I'm sorry."

Still nothing in the hallway, and he had really expected running by now if they were going to try to escape out the back way. Lane didn't strike him as the type to roll over that easily.

Behind him, he heard a gasp, so he turned to see what was going on.

The fourth girl, the short haired one who hardly spoke, was standing, and she had a gun pointed at his face.

Ethan froze. He had no idea what was going on.

Then it hit him.

Three beds.

They were only selling Max three girls. The fourth girl was a plant, probably because Lane didn't trust him.

Well, if he hadn't already been having the worst week of his life, he was now.

The other girls were skittering around, but he couldn't focus on their nervous shuffling. All he could focus on was the barrel of the gun that was pointed in his face. Not the first time he'd ever had a gun pointed at him, but definitely the first time at such close range. In such tight quarters, even if she'd never fired a gun in her life she wouldn't miss, and he was positive she had fired a gun before.

"Lane was right," she said simply, pulling back the hammer.

Ethan closed his eyes, in a split second thinking of the things he should have done differently, of the time he should've spent at home with his family—the fact that he would never see them again, never read his daughter another bed time story, tickle his giggling son or give his newborn a kiss on the forehead.

And then he heard "oomph" and several pitchy screams. He opened his eyes to see Gray Eyes standing there with the lamp in her hands, pulling back to swing again and hit the armed girl in the side of the head.

The armed girl pulled her arm up to block as she swung around, undoubtedly planning to shoot the girl who was hitting her, but Ethan sprang to life, grabbing her and getting his arm around her neck, making quick work of disarming her before anyone got shot.

The girl who had easily just saved his life skittered back, as if she hadn't just boldly attacked an armed person with nothing but a lamp. His gaze jumped to the other two girls, making sure they were okay, and there were no more decoys in the fucking bunch.

Unbelievable.

"Thanks," he muttered, unsure what the appropriate response was. Honestly, in her shoes, he might've just let the girl shoot him.

She looked a little surprised at her own actions, and she merely nodded.

Now what was he going to do with the fucking decoy? She had just heard him say who he really was—had he said his name? He didn't think he said his name, but it's not like he could change his face; if they knew to look, they could easily find him.

He never should have taken that fucking job. The money to retrieve the other girl wasn't even that good, her mother had just been such a wreck and he wanted to help.

Then he noticed the girls were looking behind him, and Lorena gasped, pointing toward the door.

When he turned, he saw Chuck standing there, a look of confusion crossing his face. "What are you doing?"

If Chuck had time to get back there, that wasn't good. Were the police not even inside yet?

He didn't have a good excuse at the ready, so he plucked the first thing he could think of out of the sky. "I was trying to… she thought I was trying to make a move or something. I don't know, man, the bitch just pulled a gun on me."

It wasn't a good excuse for so many reasons, but he couldn't think of a single solid explanation to give him on a moment's notice.

Chuck's eyes deadened. His gun was suddenly up, and he said lowly, "That's not even the one you like, Jack."

The girl he was holding onto struggled, probably trying to tell the truth, but she couldn't speak with Ethan's grip on her throat.

In the next couple of seconds, Chuck pointed his gun right at Ethan's face—the second time in the same minute, and then dumb ol' Chuck was poising to fire.

Ethan dropped his arm from around the decoy's neck and ducked, missing that bullet while the girls screamed, but Chuck was already firing again.

The decoy fell to the floor and Chuck's face fell, his gaze even angrier as he lowered his gun to where Ethan had crouched on the floor, and for the second time in as many minutes, Ethan knew he was about to die.

He heard the shots, but there was no pain. Nothing had hit him. Then he heard something heavy hit the ground and he looked up to see Chuck on the ground, his head out of view from where Ethan was at, but he wasn't moving.

The decoy was on the ground beside him, blood seeping out of her neck, her eyes open and unmoving.

"No fucking way," Ethan muttered, inching back away from her. The two Hispanic girls were huddled on a cot, each of them shielding themselves from view, one of them crying. The gray-eyed girl crouched on the floor under the other cot, her eyes huge and her face pale as she stared at the bloody young woman on the ground.

It seemed liked they all sat there frozen in time, and Ethan barely got his gun up when he heard footsteps heading toward them again. He couldn't get all the girls in one place behind him, so he hoped to God that it was the police heading back there and not Lane.

There was some urgency in the footsteps, and it sounded like at least two people. Lane and Max, or two police officers?

When the footsteps stopped outside the room, Ethan felt a hint of anticipatory relief. If it was Lane, he wouldn't have paused outside of the door, right?

And then there they were, like two beacons of light, the police, shouting at him to drop his weapon.

"They're down," he said, releasing a huge breath of relief and dropping his gun, putting his hands in the air. "I'm unarmed," he added, since presumably it was one of those guys who had just shot Chuck, and he didn't want them to be jumpy and trigger-happy while they had their weapons trained on him.

"Stand up," the one said, jerking his gun to indicate the direction, just in case Ethan didn't know which way up was.

It was over.

He glanced over at the gray-eyed girl who tentatively stood as the cops shoved him up against the lockers and cuffed him, and for a moment, he felt free.

The cuffs were a formality. Once everything was straightened out he could finally go home. Amanda would be happy to see him, Alison would run over and give him a hug,

Jackson would run over and shove his way in. He could finally hold baby Caleb again....

The second officer came in to check on the girls, and he saw the gray-eyed one go weak with relief. Then he remembered it wasn't over.

Not for him.

Not by a long shot.

His feeling of freedom dissipated as quickly as it had occurred, and as the policeman led him out of the tiny room, every last thought of the happy reunion that awaited him at home evaporated.

# Chapter Four

After Willow finished the grueling process of giving the police her statement, she was finally reunited with her family—her mom, Lauren, Ashlynn, and her brother, Todd. It was jarring having all of them there, rushing her, grabbing at her, hugging her so tightly that it hurt. Ashlynn and her mother both cried while Todd stood off to the side, hands in his pocket, shuffling his feet.

Their relief was understandable—their joy that she was even alive. It had probably been a constant fear while she was missing that they might never see her again.

Willow felt a little guilty not feeling as excited as they did, but she didn't have the energy—all she wanted was to get out of the police station and go home. She wanted to curl up in her own bed and never leave.

In the car on the way home, she sat in the back seat with Todd like they were kids again, toying with the white business card in her hands, running her fingers over the name and number of the officer in charge of her case, who had asked her to call if she remembered anything else.

Just walking into their home, Willow felt anxiety surge up inside of her. It felt like she had been away for much longer than just a few days. How could she be back so soon and yet nothing was the same as it had been when she got back from her run?

"Scott has been beside himself," Lauren told her, coming up beside her to hug her again.

Instead of returning the hug, Willow stiffened, and after a moment her mother pulled back, forcing a smile, but unable to hide the flash of hurt that grazed her features.

"I'm not up for company right now," Willow said simply.

"Oh, of course not. It's late, he can stop by tomorrow."

Another person who would ask her a million of the same questions she had already answered multiple times that night.

Since she hadn't asked any of her own, she finally asked, "Did you hire a private investigator to come get me?"

Her mother frowned, then her expression cleared. "Oh, we tried to. We called someone Ashlynn's boss knew of. We spoke to his assistant or whoever and she said she would forward the inquiry, but we never heard back from him. Why?"

Instantly regretting asking, she merely shook her head, not wanting to go into the conversation about Jack or whatever his name was.

"How did you know about that?" Ashlynn insisted, a frown marring her brow.

Sighing in defeat, she said, "He was there, I guess. That's what he said anyway, I didn't know if he was lying, or…telling the truth. I thought he was lying but he knew both of your names."

For the next several minutes that was all they talked about, excitedly speculating about the situation and trying to pry more details out of her. She felt like they viewed her experience like an episode of Law and Order, and that pissed her off. When she couldn't take anymore, she told them she needed to go take a long, hot shower, and the two older women exchanged looks. Her mom nodded slightly and Ashlynn asked if she could talk to her for a moment alone; Willow was pretty sure she knew what was coming.

Back in her youth—long, long ago—Ashlynn had worked on a volunteer basis with some rape crisis center. Being that Willow was a girl, essentially sold—at least she thought?—to a brothel-owner after being held by criminals for several days and rescued in terribly scanty clothing, it was not at all outside the realm of logic to wonder if she had been raped. Every girl in that room with Willow had been raped—

the main reason, she suspected, that the police officer had looked slightly confused when she insisted that she hadn't.

Just thinking about it made her want to throw up, and she didn't have it in her to go through that for the second time in one night.

"I'd really rather not, not tonight," Willow said, shaking her head. "I'm fine, I just want a shower."

Turning to head up the stairs, she barely made it to the top before she heard footsteps behind her. Sighing irritably, she went into her room, pausing for a moment to look at it, just as she'd left it. Tears welled up behind her eyes and she didn't even know why, but she ignored them, walking over to her dresser and pulling out clothes to change into.

Ashlynn paused in the doorway, her long salt and pepper brown hair pulled into a low pony tail, hanging over her shoulder. Her brown eyes bore the distinct look of concern.

"I need to talk to you before you get into the shower, honey."

"I'm all talked out, Ashlynn."

Technically, Ashlynn was like a mother to her; she had been with Lauren since Willow was four, but she didn't refer to Ashlynn that way.

"Honey... I just... please sit down with me for a minute."

Willow closed her eyes for a moment, her back still to Ashlynn, and searched for the strength to do it all over again. Her concerns were understandable, but Willow needed her to just leave it alone. In an attempt to put them off, she insisted she would talk the next day, but she knew she wouldn't—not about that.

Even Willow couldn't figure out how to feel about it, and she had been the one who endured all of it.

"I can't help noticing you didn't need to go to the hospital after you left the police station."

"Nope," Willow said simply. "Uninjured. No need."

"If they hurt you while you were there, it's best to go to the doctor *before* you take a shower. I know you just want to scrub everything away and climb into bed, but... if you decide later—"

"I don't need to go to the hospital, Ashlynn. I'm completely fine, I'm just dirty and tired and I saw a woman be *murdered* tonight, so I really just want to get clean and try to get some sleep."

Ashlynn hesitated, then said, "If you *were* hurt a shower will probably wash away the evidence."

"I wasn't," Willow insisted. "Now please, let me take a shower."

"If you were though, you know you know it wasn't your fault, right?"

"Yes," she said shortly.

"Even if... if it was more than one, especially then—"

"Ashlynn!" Willow interrupted, her eyes widening. "I don't want to talk about this."

Ashlynn looked a bit wounded, but she went on, "If they did though, they deserve to be punished. You know that, right?"

That was the question that held her up. The other responses had been simple, tossed out there without having to run them through her brain first; she had been prepared for those questions.

After a hesitation that lasted far too long, Willow managed a nod. "Yeah, I know," she said with decidedly less hostility. "I do. I'm just tired, okay?"

"If you ever need... to talk to me, you have my confidence. I won't even tell your mother if you don't want me to."

"I appreciate that," Willow said, and she meant it, even if she didn't have the energy to convey sincerity in that moment.

"And if you did want to go to the hospital—just to be safe—you could change your mind later. Going to the hospital doesn't mean you have to pursue it, but... tonight is your best—maybe your only—shot at physical evidence if you decide you *do* have something else to report."

"I'm fine," Willow said again, shoving her dresser drawer shut.

Ashlynn nodded sadly, and Willow made a beeline for her bathroom, closing and locking the door, then leaning against it and closing her eyes.

*I'm fine*, she repeated, that time in her head, only for herself.

After she stripped off her clothes and turned on the shower to warm up, Willow looked at her naked body in the mirror. There were a few bruises here and there, but nothing to indicate what she had gone through. Nothing to indicate she was any different.

Foolish tears began to well up again so she turned to test the water and stepped into the shower. She pulled the curtain closed, hugging herself, squeezing her eyes shut as the water beat down on her. Behind her eyelids—images of everything that had happened that night, the dead girl bleeding all over the cold floor, the PI nearly being shot in the face. The split second before she grabbed the lamp, when she considered letting it happen. The fear coursing through her veins when she turned on Willow, and it occurred to her that attacking someone with a gun with a *lamp* probably wasn't the best idea. The PI awkwardly thanking her. The discomfort of realizing she had risked her own life to save her rapist.

She opened her eyes.

• • •
*50*

The water wasn't hot enough—she wanted it to be scalding—so she turned a little more heat on and waited, flinching when the water made it through the pipes and started hitting her. After a moment, her body adjusted to the heat and she turned around, wanting it to wash over every inch of her.

There was a purple loofah hanging off the shower hook—the same one she had used before—and she grabbed it, pouring way too much soap on and then rubbing it, lathering it up. She dragged it over her skin roughly, not satisfied until every square inch was red and agitated, and really not even satisfied then. As she washed between her legs, she was hit with a flash of that night, the man's hands on her hips, on her butt, between her legs… There was a quickening in her chest, a fluttering of nerves. She couldn't think about that. She scrubbed and scrubbed, but there was no scrubbing her brain. Even opening her eyes didn't help that time. The mental image was gone, seeing the audience watching her be assaulted, nobody lifting a finger to help. But the memory was there, whether her eyes were open or closed. The one called Chuck squeezing her breast, trying to entice the other one to rape her.

The pain when he pushed past her hymen.

The blood on her thighs as she tried to will herself to go to sleep that night.

It was all too much. Part of her wanted to get out of the shower to get away from the thoughts, but it wasn't the shower, it was her mind, and she couldn't get out of that.

At least in the shower, her tears were washed away as quickly as they fell, so it felt less like crying.

She tried to refocus her attention, to think of anything else. She even grabbed her shampoo bottle and read the directions on the back just to keep her mind occupied, but since it was the last thing she wanted to relive, her brain kept going back to it.

After running out all of the hot water, she knew she had to get out.

When she did, she wished she hadn't looked in the mirror. Her eyes were bloodshot, red-rimmed from crying, and her face was a puffy mess.

She hoped Ashlynn wasn't still sitting outside waiting for her.

Somehow the smaller space of the bathroom felt safer than the bedroom. It was only her bathroom, no one else ever came in there, so instead of returning to her bedroom, after she finished pulling clothes on with considerable effort, and brushing her teeth until her gums bled, she sat down in the corner, leaned against the tub and the wall, and pulled her knees up to her chest, pulling her body in as much as she could.

She just wasn't ready to face the world.

She leaned forward, burying her face in her arms, and welcoming the quiet, dark bubble that she felt like she had enveloped herself in.

She wished that she could stay in the bathroom until everything was back to normal.

But she wasn't sure anything would ever be normal again.

# CHAPTER FIVE

When Ethan woke up in his own bed with his wife curled up beside him, he thought for a moment he was dreaming.

Even after realizing he was awake, it still felt as reliable as a dream.

When the police had released him, he had been genuinely confused. Relieved, but confused. He wasn't sure how or why, but as he high-tailed it out of the police station, he hadn't questioned his luck.

Rolling over, he spotted the baby's pack-n-play over by Amanda's side of the bed, his son happily snoozing, his little face so peaceful.

*I shouldn't be here*, he thought. Couldn't *help* thinking it.

He actually hadn't dreamed about it that night, but he'd thought about what he had done before he fell asleep, reliving it all in his mind as Amanda nursed the baby at 3 am. There, in the familiarity of his bed, there was a level of disbelief that hadn't been there before.

He could not *believe* what he had done. It didn't feel real.

But the memories did.

The girl on her knees in front of him, bent over and crying, the bloody condom. Not nice mental pictures.

Willow.

That was her name.

He checked after he got home.

He wished he didn't know her name. Knowing nothing about her was a little easier. As just one of several nameless girls being trafficked into prostitution, she had no specific humanness, no details of who she was as a person. Obviously he had felt terrible about it, but in the counterculture he had been immersed in, in that situation, even though he wasn't *really* Jack and didn't *actually* take part in that kind of life, it was easier to swallow. It was almost normal behavior; he knew anyone around him would have done the same thing.

Back in the ranks of decent humanity where only wicked people did something like that to someone else, it was much harder. Knowing that Willow had two parents—or three, he still hadn't checked into her father yet—and a brother who loved her, knowing that one week earlier she had probably been an innocent teenage girl with hobbies and crushes and dreams of her own… Ethan felt sick just thinking about it.

In 10 years, his own daughter would be Willow's age, with her own hopes and dreams, and if anyone ever did anything to break her, he wouldn't even hesitate to kill them with his bare hands.

He'd never had anything to be deeply ashamed of before. One week earlier, he slept well at night and wouldn't have felt guilty when his wife gave him a good night kiss.

Amanda. It seemed like they'd been together forever—since college, anyway. She was a year younger, graduated a year later, but she was the most beautiful woman he had ever seen. Long black hair, beautiful blue eyes, and the first time he saw her in her favorite black dress, he knew his single days were over.

She still had that dress. Still brought it out on special occasions. When he returned home, she demanded a date night. She hadn't lost her baby weight from Caleb yet, so she wouldn't be able to wear the dress, or that would have been one of those occasions.

He didn't care, she was beautiful no matter what she wore, no matter how much she weighed.

And he could hardly stand to look at her with the guilt of what he'd done weighing on his conscience.

The baby started to fuss once he woke up, and Amanda grumbled and buried her face in the pillow, so Ethan smiled a little and dragged himself out of bed.

Lifting his son out of his bassinet, he brushed a kiss across his forehead and brought him to his shoulder. "Hey there, little buddy," he whispered, quietly walking to the door and easing it open.

The baby's head bobbed a bit unsteadily but Ethan put his hand behind his head so he didn't get too crazy.

"You're going to spend a little time with Daddy right now, okay? We're going to let Mommy sleep."

Caleb didn't seem entirely on board with that plan, as he started rooting for Ethan's chest.

"Ah, sorry, nothing's coming out of there, bud."

After a diaper change, he went to the kitchen to get a bottle ready, checking his email while he waited. He wasn't going into the office until later, but he should probably call his assistant and see if the Torres family had made their payment yet.

Their daughter was returned to them in the same condition as Willow, but at least in her case, he wasn't the one who caused it.

He should also look into whether or not Willow's father was really Antonio Castellanos. And then maybe look into relocating if he was.

---

The day after she got home, Willow got a new phone. When she was abducted, the phone had been in her pocket, and no one knew or cared where that was anymore.

Unfortunately, a means of communication with the outside world was the last thing on Willow's mind. As soon as her number was working again, there was an outpouring of "support" from all of her friends, family, and people she had met once or twice several years earlier. She wasn't sure why they thought she'd want to be pestered all day long, or why that was even considered supportive, but apparently people thought it would make her feel better. Then there were the people who were just blatantly curious about the details of her ordeal, and several who were apparently unaware of how inconsiderate it was to come out and ask those questions. As if she wanted to keep thinking about it.

Some reporter from the local paper had already called that morning, wanting to do a story about her.

A local business sent over an edible arrangement.

The neighbors took turns knocking on the door.

The oddest thing people felt the need to tell her was, "We're so happy you're home safe."

Why would she think they *wouldn't* want her to return home safely? Hoping for that outcome was a pretty normal response, so she wasn't sure it needed to be remarked on, and she had no idea what to say back. Thanks? Thanks for preferring that I remain alive?

By the end of the day, she felt like a sideshow, and she turned her phone off to avoid the temptation of habitually checking it every time it went off.

Scott had been up her ass since she got back, too. Normally he wasn't a clinger, but apparently having your girlfriend abducted by a group of criminals made you appreciate what you had. When he couldn't get her on her phone after an hour, he resorted to calling the house phone; when she ignored that, he decided to just stop over.

She knew she couldn't put him off forever, but she had been hoping for one more day before she had to face him.

Things had been awkward at first, probably because her attitude made them that way. In no way did she attempt to hide her exhaustion with people by the time he got there, so when he offered his own appreciation that she was alive, she had no polite responses left, and didn't say a single word.

If he would have waited, given her time, maybe she would've been happy to see him.

Since he did not, his presence was about as welcome as a mosquito's, and she went to no lengths to pretend otherwise.

Especially when he went fishing for information with the enormously unsubtle remark, "I heard sometimes when girls are taken by people like that, they do really bad things to them."

"Really?" she shot back, her eyes going wide as she mockingly dropped her jaw open. "I always heard they took them out to fancy dinners!"

Properly admonished, he merely added that if she needed to talk or anything, his mom knew a good shrink.

She thought it was nice that his mom's therapist would listen to her ails, but he didn't offer to.

Of course, she resented people who offered to lend an ear as well, so maybe she was just pissed off at the whole world and it didn't matter what he said.

After he left, she masochistically went through the news articles related to her, but after reading many of the comments, she was more irritated than she had been when she started.

As long as the list of well-wishers was that day, her father's name was not on it. That infuriated her, too, even though she should be used to it. On her father's priority list, her name fell somewhere around the middle of the third page. Maybe closer to the bottom if he had other love children that he liked more, which was quite possible.

When Scott finally left, Willow changed into her pajamas and climbed into bed, but as tired as she was, she couldn't sleep. She was completely consumed with fear.

The night before, by the time she made it to bed, she told herself there would be no nightmares. She was back in the comfort of her own bed, and the nightmare that had been her reality for several days could no longer touch her, not if she didn't let it.

When she awoke at 4 am, her gaze jumping fearfully around the room, convinced that she was back in that awful place, the only thing that kept her from crawling out of her bed and into a corner somewhere was her sudden, all-consuming terror of the dark. Even though she knew logically that if she pushed back her covers and climbed out of bed, there would be no sleeping girls laying there, no sleazy monster with a gun to torment her, she couldn't rely on that logic.

Emotionally, she was wrecked. All she could do was lie there, paralyzed with fear, with the covers pulled up to her neck. She stared at the ceiling and fought to regain control over her own thoughts.

It didn't work.

For the next four hours, she stayed like that, her heavy eyelids refusing to close, with real memories and memories of her nightmares rolling through her mind. Knowing that it wasn't real and that no one could really hurt her anymore didn't help at all.

Then her thoughts of what could have happened kicked into high gear. Imagining what it would have been like if the police wouldn't have busted the place, if she would have been forced into prostitution. What would her nightmares have been like then? Probably nothing that could have rivaled her reality.

She felt so disconnected from everyone in her life. As much as they cared, as much as they loved her, none of them had experienced what she had. None of them knew anything about the kind of people who had stolen control of her fate. They didn't know how she felt, lying on a shared mattress in a dark room with other women, knowing that they were all being processed like cattle. The whole time, feeling like it couldn't possibly be real, because things like that could never happen to someone like her. She was normal. She had a family, a life, people who missed her. Things like that couldn't happen to girls like her.

Except that it did.

But one week earlier, she wouldn't have been able to understand either.

Nobody in her life understood, because nobody else was there.

Never before had more people showered her with offers of love and support, and never before in her life had she felt so alone.

# CHAPTER SIX

It had been one week since Willow had been abducted.

Her mother, armed with research she had done online, suggested that Willow go to her tennis lesson that day, telling her that doing things she had done *before* would help her.

That was how she referred to it, just before.

While Ashlynn was more grounded in reality and wanted to face the issues head on and deal with them, Lauren was happy to live in denial, and as long as Willow wanted to insist that nothing bad had happened to her, Lauren would happily go on believing it.

Given Willow's silence on the matter anytime either of her mothers attempted to delve for information about Ethan's role in her rescue, she figured it was probably her own fault when her mother happily announced at lunch time that the man who was responsible for Willow's rescue would be joining them for dinner that evening.

"What?" Willow demanded, not prepared for the news, so unable to hide her dismay.

Ashlynn seemed surprised by it, but Lauren remained mostly oblivious, although her smile faltered a bit at her daughter's tone. "Well, he has to get his check… I thought it would be a nice way to thank him."

Willow's whole body went so rigid that she thought she might crack in half. "You're paying him?"

Ashlynn frowned and opened her mouth to say something, but before she could, Lauren said, "Well, yes, of course. I mean, he was the one working with the cops that night, and we contacted his office about taking the case, so it only seems right. I guess since he never technically got back to us… but that seems unfair. He put himself at great risk from what I understand, and we would've paid 20 times that amount if we could have."

The initial shock had worn off, and she had enough time to get herself under control, but she couldn't muster a very good performance, so she retreated to her bedroom.

Once there, she didn't know what to do with herself. The last thing she needed was time to think, but being around her family was grating on her nerves. It was early so it was still light outside, but she turned the light on anyway and climbed into bed.

Somehow she needed to mentally prepare herself for dinner. She had no idea how she was supposed to sit across from him after what he had done and pretend like nothing happened. Pretend to be *grateful*. Her heart raced thinking about it alone in her room, when she wasn't looking at his face. How would she be able to think of anything else? How would she be able to force down the food with memories of being on her knees before him, having to force *him* down her throat? Without thinking about the pain, the anguish, that his actions had caused her?

Even if he didn't want to do it.

That was the real kicker. The pain was real, the anxiety was real, the memories were real, his was the face she had to pin it on, but… he hadn't wanted to do it. There had been no malicious intent. *He* wasn't trying to take away her control, her ability to say no, he was merely the tool that Lane used to do it. Physically he had forced himself on her, but he didn't really have a choice, and that made it so much more confusing.

Also, if he wouldn't have been there, she would be forcibly whored out to all manner of disgusting men. Instead of one man forcing himself on her, how many would there have been at that point? Four? Ten? More than that? Her dream from the night before wouldn't just be a nightmare, it would be her life.

If he wouldn't have been there, she didn't know if she would have ever made it home.

Not to mention, he had almost been shot himself while saving her.

And yet, she still wasn't sure she could stand to look at him across the dinner table without betraying her discomfort.

Why had her stupid mother invited him to dinner?

---

When Ethan pulled into the Kensington driveway, he just sat there for a moment, gripping the steering wheel so hard that his hands hurt.

He had tried all day to prepare himself. He was doing *exactly* what he'd been determined not to do—giving himself more evidence of the gray-eyed girl's humanity.

When her mother called his office to talk to him, he'd felt a deep sense of foreboding. Maybe Willow hadn't gone to the police, but she had probably come clean with her own mom. He had been braced for an audible bomb when he picked up the phone.

Instead he got a dinner invite.

Despite the several excuses he gave her in quick succession, she insisted that what he did meant so much to her family and she was more grateful than she could ever express, and she practically *begged* him to come over for a thank-you dinner.

He wasn't sure how much dinner he would be able to eat, as sick as he felt.

Since he really, really did not want to go, he made one last attempt, telling her that he wasn't sure it would be good for her daughter, seeing as he had been posing as one of the bad guys during her captivity, so just seeing him might make her relive what had happened to her.

That was a very real concern for him, but the woman on the other end of the line did not seem to be capable of processing that possibility. She called that suggestion "absurd" and added that Willow was so grateful for what he had done, and she was sure that Willow would want him to come.

He was 100% sure that she was wrong, but she sounded so sure of herself, even he almost believed it for a second.

So there he stood, waiting outside their house for the ground to open up and swallow him so he didn't have to walk through those doors and lay eyes on the one person in the world he never wanted to see again.

He could already feel his face heating up, and he suspected it was not because of the weather. He had no idea how he was going to get through dinner.

The perky one, Lauren, greeted him at the door, actually pulling him into a hug that made him feel immensely uncomfortable. He made the mistake of looking past her, and immediately noticed a pair of gray eyes boring into him, like little daggers. He awkwardly pulled back from the hug and attempted some semblance of a smile for her mother's benefit, but smiling in front of the girl, trying to pretend everything was okay seemed so wrong. She should know that he didn't take her feelings lightly, that he had done her a terrible wrong and that he didn't deserve thankful hugs from her mother. And she deserved to know that *he* knew that.

How he could possibly express that to her, he had no idea, but he knew it wasn't through fake smiles and bullshitting with her parents as if he deserved their admiration.

The whole situation was extremely unfair to her, and he had no idea how to change that short of coming clean, which he was not about to do.

Taking care of his family had to come before relieving his own conscience.

Before dinner, Lauren brought out the reward check and tried to give it to him. She hadn't said anything on the phone about the check, and since he hadn't formally been hired, he hadn't been expecting one. Honestly, finding Willow had happened purely by accident; he hadn't been looking for her.

"Oh, no," he said, not taking the check. "No, no. You can keep that."

Since he looked at the check like it was on fire, the more reasonable mother was understandably flummoxed.

"Why? This is what you get paid for, isn't it?"

The girl was sitting as far away from him as she could, staring down at her hands, refusing to be mentally present. Couldn't blame her there.

"It is, but I didn't actually take your case. I wasn't there to get your daughter. Obviously I'm glad that she was brought back home to you, but I was working someone else's case; honestly, even if you wouldn't have contacted me, she would've been returned to you. I wouldn't feel right taking your money."

The woman nodded as if she accepted his answer, but he couldn't shake the feeling that she was suspicious of him. Maybe it was just his own guilty conscience, but he was already counting down the seconds until he could leave.

Throughout dinner, Ethan awkwardly made conversation with her parents, and the girl was silent unless someone forced her to talk.

It was a painfully uncomfortable situation, and he felt like the longer he sat there, the more damage he was doing. So he ate as quickly as he could, and Lauren did most of the talking while he uttered suitably polite responses. When he finally shoveled the last bite into his mouth, he intended to get the hell out of there, but he noticed that no one else had finished.

Waiting for everyone else to finish was excruciating.

Especially Willow, who had barely touched her food.

Everybody *but* Willow had finished and she showed no signs of finishing soon, so he finally said fuck manners and took the customary breath of someone who regretted what they were about to say.

"Well, I appreciate the meal, but I should really be getting home now."

"Oh, but we haven't had dessert yet," Lauren said, her eyes darting into the kitchen. "You have to stay for dessert, it's one of Willow's recipes. She's quite the cook, you know, always trying out some new recipe."

Of course he hadn't known, and he wished he didn't. He didn't want to know what her hobbies were, or anything else that would make him feel worse than he already did.

It was bad enough *seeing* her in her home with her family, looking every bit the teenage girl she was. It made him feel lower than he had before. He was 32 years old, for fuck's sake. She had just turned 18. He was almost old enough to be her father, and he suddenly couldn't look at her across the table without seeing her on her knees in front of him, her mouth slightly swollen, her eyes red from crying...

He felt disgusting. He felt like a monster. He couldn't have felt worse if he had hurt her because he *wanted* to.

He was fighting images of Willow with a gun to her temple, bending to take his cock in her mouth, and her mother was sitting there trying to feed him dessert while Willow had to sit there silently and take it.

Clearing his throat, he abruptly pushed his chair back. "No, thank you, I really have to go."

After offering one more time to wrap him up some to take home, Lauren smiled graciously and said, "Well, okay. Thank you from the bottom of my heart for helping my daughter return home safely. I can't tell you how grateful we all are."

Barely managing not to flinch, he nodded and thanked her again for dinner.

"Willow will walk you out," Lauren volunteered.

"Lauren," Ashlynn snapped, obviously the only one of the two to notice how uncomfortable Willow was.

Willow pushed back her chair, standing. "It's fine."

Avoiding looking at her more suspicious mother, Ethan nodded once politely and kept his head down, falling into step behind Willow.

With his head down like that, he couldn't help looking at her ass as she walked in front of him.

Self-disgust washed over him as he quickly averted his gaze.

Willow opened the door, and when he looked up at her hesitantly, as if he wanted to speak, she stepped outside with him, closing the door behind her. Then she crossed her arms across her chest and looked up at him expectantly.

"Thank you," he said simply.

She merely shrugged, looking out at the lawn instead of at him. "No point ruining your life. One of the other goons would have done it anyway."

He looked down, at a loss for what to say. "I'm so, so sorry. I know that I hurt you in a way that…that no one can ever fix, and I can't imagine that keeping it all inside is making this any easier on you. If there's anything I can ever do..."

She shook her head, but he noticed she still wouldn't look at him. "I'm fine," she said simply.

"I'm not," he said honestly, "so I don't see how you could be."

That time she met his gaze, and in that short-lived moment, he saw a glimpse of her anguish, but she quickly looked away. "You didn't really have a choice."

"That doesn't change what happened to you."

The girl swallowed, still looking away, then she swallowed again, and he wondered if she was having a hard time keeping her composure. Finally, she met his eyes, and he saw that hers were shining. "Thank you for saying that."

He nodded, since he wasn't sure what to say.

The girl cleared her throat, blinking a little more rapidly than was normal. "You could've taken the money."

"Wouldn't have been right," he said simply.

She nodded, understanding better than anyone else could why he felt that way. "Well, I should go back inside."

He nodded in rhythm with her bobbing head, both of them clearly uncomfortable. He was glad she was the one to initiate his exit, because he didn't know how to walk away from her. "Yeah, I should go, too."

"Right. Wife and three kids."

It felt like an accusation, even though he knew it wasn't one. He didn't say anything, merely nodded again.

Absently hooking her fingers in the back pockets of her jeans, she said, "Well, I'll let you get back to that."

He still didn't feel comfortable leaving, but he felt just as uncomfortable standing there, so he finally bit the bullet and turned around, making his way down the front porch steps.

Before he made it off the last step, he found himself turning to see if she was still there.

She had turned and had her hand on the doorknob when he called out.

She stopped, hesitantly turning in his direction.

"I meant… what I said. If you ever think of anything I can do for you…"

She probably knew as well as he did there wasn't much he could do for her—unless she wanted dirt on her boyfriend or something—but she nodded anyway. "My mom has your number."

He couldn't say why, but he found himself reaching into his pocket and pulling out a card. Then he found himself jotting his cell number on the back. He went back up the stairs and offered it to her.

"Just in case."

She merely stared at the card, not moving to take it. "I don't have a lot of use for private investigators, believe it or not."

"Right," he said, feeling stupid.

He just wished there was *something* he could do to take away even a fraction of the pain she had to be feeling.

Even though he knew it was probably even dumber, he added, "If you ever need to talk to someone who knows what happened…I'm the last person who would try to defend myself or anyone else involved."

For a few seconds, she just stared at him, but then she reached for the card. "I highly doubt I'll ever use it, but… just in case."

He nodded once, his mouth curving up grimly, then he made his way back down the steps without turning back.

"Do you have any daughters?" she called out.

He stopped, flinching a little. "Yeah."

She didn't say anything else, and a moment later he heard the door close, so he suspected she only asked in case he hadn't thought about it.

As if he could ever *stop* thinking about it.

Making his way back to his car, he figured that if the little dig made her feel even fractionally better, it was worth it. He would stand there and let her fling pure venom at him if it would make her feel even a little bit better.

Perhaps the flagellation would make *him* feel better. Knowing that she had to lie to her family and remain silent about what happened to her really ate away at him. He *knew* that was unhealthy. Having grown up with a physically abusive father of his own and a mother who was more concerned with keeping the family secrets than her own child's well-being, he knew just how much her silence was costing her.

And she shouldn't be the one paying.

# CHAPTER SEVEN

Before Ethan's car made it out of the driveway, Ashlynn was staring Willow down with a look of determination all over her face.

Intending to evade the coming onslaught, Willow said she was going upstairs.

When she made it to her bedroom alone, she thought she was safe—until she heard footsteps on the stairs. A moment later, Ashlynn stood in her doorway.

"You seemed incredibly uncomfortable the whole time he was here."

"Yeah, well… it's not like we share great memories."

That was true. It wasn't the truth, but it *was* true.

Ashlynn stepped inside, closing the door behind her. Slowly approaching Willow, she glanced at the bed—unmade—and asked, "May I sit?"

Sighing audibly, Willow said, "I can't stop you."

Ashlynn glanced down, but took a seat on the edge of the bed anyway. "Did your mother ever tell you about my childhood?"

"No."

"It wasn't a good one. A close friend of the family... well, let's just say he wasn't as trustworthy as my family thought he was."

Willow squirmed, but said nothing.

"When he would come over, I behaved the way you just did. Silent, angry, repressed, resentful... It wasn't fair that I had to pretend everything was all right when it wasn't. It wasn't fair that my parents were nice to him, that they even *spoke* to him after what he had done to me. It made me feel terrible."

"That sucks," Willow muttered, feeling she should acknowledge what Ashlynn had experienced, but not wanting to feed her imagination either.

"Yes, it did suck." Ashlynn paused. "That man, the PI, he was living as one of them, wasn't he?"

"Yes," Willow ground out, not wanting to think about it.

More hesitantly, Ashlynn asked, "Did he hurt you?"

Willow shook her head, not able to get the word out. "He wasn't one of the bad guys, he was just pretending to be."

"That's not what I asked," she replied gingerly.

"He almost died," Willow stated, finally looking over at the other woman. "Do you know that? He almost died because I wouldn't listen when he told me to do something, so he blew his cover to convince me, and one of the girls in the room was a spy. She had a gun. She almost shot him in the face. You have no idea what we went through, either one of us. I'm sorry that I'm not as gregarious as I was before, but I spent days locked up in a dark room with no idea what was going to happen to me, and I don't *feel* great about it. I'm back now, it's over for you guys, but it isn't over for me. I'm not ready to be around people yet, I'm pissed off at everyone who so much as looks at me, and I don't know why. I don't know why I feel this way, I can't just turn it off, but seeing him—it just makes me think about what I went through, okay? Maybe he's used to doing stuff like that so he could recover faster, be polite, but I don't have it in me. I don't give a damn what anybody thinks of me right now. I don't give a *fuck* if people think I'm being rude or antisocial, to be *perfectly* honest."

Ashlynn nodded, averting her gaze. "I just… don't know how to help you."

Laughing joylessly, Willow said, "Join the club."

Appearing to be at a loss for words, Ashlynn just sat there, sadly gazing at the carpet.

For a second, Willow felt bad for snapping at her, but then she told herself to stop. It was not her job to babysit anyone else. *She* was going through something, and if she needed space, they needed to give it to her.

After a minute, Ashlynn slowly rose, simply asking that Willow come talk to her if she needed to, even if she wanted Ashlynn to just listen and not speak. Willow told her she would, succinctly thanked her, and then closed the door behind her.

---

It had been three weeks since Willow's homecoming.

Despite the wishes of her family, she did not magically recover once she had some time to "digest" everything that had happened.

Although she wasn't sure it was the right thing to do, Willow attempted to track the case to find out what would happen to the people who had kidnapped her.

Honestly, she was just trying to figure out why it had happened. Why her? Just because of who her father was? She knew so little of his world that she wasn't even sure how important he was, and she definitely didn't know why it had happened, why they thought she would be a good way to get to him, if that was the case.

A little over a week after she was home safe, her father had sent over a vase full of flowers with an iTunes gift card where most people put a little note card.

The articles online weren't very helpful. It seemed like nothing had changed, and she didn't see how that could be true. They were obviously very dangerous men who stole *people* and sold them like old clothes. She may not know a lot about the law but she did know that was not okay, and there must be extremely harsh punishments coming their way.

The one they called Tito was never mentioned in the articles, at least not by that name. There were a couple of names she didn't recognize though, so she thought Tito might be a nickname.

There were still articles about her online, and they had attached pictures, which she didn't appreciate. Not like everyone at her school didn't know what had happened to her—or some version of it anyway—but having her face plastered all over the internet so some douche named Bob in Nebraska could remark on how he'd like to kidnap her, too…oddly enough, it didn't help.

The article contained lines like "the family is asking for privacy at this time," and "the police have declined to discuss specifics of the investigation." There were some generally nice comments, offering thoughts and prayers, then one guy talking about if she would have had a gun, that wouldn't have happened to her; some unhappy looking woman commenting that she was probably in on it and lying, because she looked like a criminal, and because the photo they chose to use of her in that article showed her in a mini-skirt (which seemed like an odd choice, given that she could count on one hand how many photos there were of her in a mini-skirt); one asshole saying they probably just thought she was a hooker and they should "go easy" on the guys; another valiant gentleman remarking "I bet she got gangbanged."

There were more comments, but Willow was too thoroughly disgusted with humanity to read any more of them.

Just because she knew herself well enough to know she would look it up again later out of morbid curiosity, she crawled under her desk and unplugged the power cord.

When she first got back, her friends were all eager to show their support. As time passed and she failed to return to normal or "get over it," they began to lose interest. Their lives hadn't changed, but Willow had, so they started calling less and less.

Her boyfriend was the only exception, and it seemed that nobody in the world annoyed her more than he did. Mostly she suspected it was because he seemed desperate to pretend that it hadn't happened and everything was normal, and she couldn't do that.

Consequently, she spent a lot of time by herself. The temptation to look up articles on her phone was still there, and seeing her friends leaving inane comments and statuses all over the place was frustrating her, too, so she finally just turned the internet off her phone altogether.

She could feel herself withdrawing from everything. Her tennis lessons had gone on without her, because she never went back. She didn't care about any of the things she had cared about when she left—that would require caring about *something*, and she didn't.

More time than she expected was devoted to reliving what had happened, piece by piece, every single day. Even when she slept, different versions of the same things would happen, sometimes mixing in people that she knew in real life, sometimes sticking to the real cast of characters. The previous night, she had dreamed of watching Ethan make out with one of the other girls, wanting to tell them not to do it, but she had no voice and no real reason to tell the girl what to do, other than the fact that she considered it unwise.

It was still difficult to think about the sex. She didn't want to think of it as anything else—didn't want to think of it at all, but she couldn't help it.

Since she hadn't reported it, she hadn't gone to the hospital for any testing. He had used a condom, plus he was married, so she assumed he hadn't given her any diseases.

It wasn't like she would be having sex with anyone anytime soon anyway, so she saw no urgent need to ensure her sexual health. Logically, she knew that she should go get checked out, but the idea of going to a gynecologist and having someone poking and prodding at her made her feel senselessly rebellious.

It was one thing she could control, and as stupid as it seemed, she didn't care.

She felt like her life was never going to be normal again. Like *she* was never going to be normal again. And not even knowing who to blame did *not* help matters. Sometimes she felt angry at Ethan; other times, after thinking it over, she felt like he had been a victim, too. The latter made her feel worse, so she tried to think of him as a bad guy, just without intent.

It was very complicated, but it made her feel like she had some power, choosing whether or not to forgive him.

Her mothers were on opposite sides of the reaction spectrum. Lauren was determined to remain cheerful and positive, ignoring Willow's surly moods and trying to cycle through all of the suggestions she had read about in some online article about how to reclaim your life after surviving a kidnapping. Instead of dealing with it, she wanted to distract Willow, to sweep her up in the present in some foolhardy expectation that one night in the city going to dinner and seeing one of Willow's favorite plays might simply wipe her memory, at least for the night.

When it didn't, the ride home was quiet, Lauren's disappointment palpable.

It made Willow feel even worse.

Instead of trying to ignore everything that happened and get Willow back to doing the things she used to enjoy, Ashlynn suggested the opposite. After the dinner with Ethan, Ashlynn became very pushy about Willow seeing a counselor. Willow resisted. She went on to suggest maybe Willow should try something new to get out of the house—not her old activities, but something completely different. Maybe a kick-boxing class or Zumba.

Needless to say, Willow didn't want do any of that, but the weight of their expectations grew heavier each day.

Then one night Scott wanted to come over for dinner and bring one of her favorite movies to watch. The bastard was smart enough to suggest that before leaving, standing inside the house within earshot of Lauren. So when Willow said she wasn't up for it, her mother came in and insisted, saying that sounded nice, and reassuring Willow that she would love it, that it would be just like before.

As Willow sat on her bed, watching the movie resentfully, she did not love it. Not at all.

"You don't seem like you're enjoying the movie," Scott remarked.

"I *told* you I didn't want to watch it. My mom is the one who thought this was a good idea; maybe you should go watch the movie with her."

"Why are you being like this?" he responded, scowling.

Willow's eyes went wide and she stared at him for a second. "Are you serious?"

He sighed, raking a hand through his chestnut hair. "Okay, forget it. I'm sorry, I shouldn't have said that."

Since apparently the thing to do after a not-quite-fight and failed at-home-date was to make out, Scott went for it. It was brave enough that she let it go, plus she figured if she kissed him for a few minutes he might be satisfied and he'd go home.

For a moment, the thought pained her; before she was taken, she had *liked* Scott. A lot. Getting a text or a call from him had elicited a girly smile; she enjoyed running her fingers through his hair while they kissed, and she would have loved to curl up in her bed and watch a movie while cuddling with him.

She didn't know why she seemed to resent him so much; he hadn't *done* anything.

Of course, realizing how little control she still had over her emotions did not put her in the mood for kissing, so when his hand slipped between her legs without any encouragement on her end, she clenched her legs together in hopes that he would get the message.

He didn't.

And she was wearing a fucking dress.

So while she waited for him to realize she was saying no and pull back, he plodded on ahead, somehow ignorant of the meaning of her leg clenching, until his finger slipped up under her underwear.

"Stop it," she finally murmured, feeling slightly pissed off that he wasn't taking her nonverbal cues.

Whether he didn't hear her or for some reason just didn't take her seriously, he did not stop. His stupid mouth was on her neck and his finger clumsily attempted to push inside of her. Once she felt the intrusion, she shoved him away with considerable force.

He caught himself, scowling at her as if in confusion. "What?"

"What the hell is wrong with you? I said stop!"

Looking all put out, Scott said, "What?"

"I told you to stop."

"I wasn't doing anything!"

Willow rolled her eyes and climbed off the bed, not even wanting to be near him.

"Willow, what's going on with you? Ever since you've been back, you've been...so different."

"Yeah, well, I wasn't on a fucking Caribbean cruise, now, was I?"

She heard the bed creak behind her, indicating he had climbed off the bed as well, and she tensed in anticipation of him being stupid enough to try to touch her.

"You said you were fine."

He was right, she did say that, all the time; since she had returned home, it was basically her mantra.

And he didn't see through it. Even though it probably wasn't fair, she resented him for that.

"I think you should go home," she said, fiddling with the bottles of nail polish lined up on her dresser instead of looking at him.

"You don't even want to hang out now?"

"No, I don't want to hang out at all, to be perfectly honest. You don't get it, and I'm not going to spoon feed it to you, so... I think you should just go."

"Are you breaking up with me?" he asked in disbelief. "Willow, just tell me what I did wrong. I won't do it again. I wasn't trying to piss you off, I was just trying to be affectionate with my girlfriend."

Rounding on him, she said more loudly than she intended, "Yeah, well, I don't *want* your affection. I just want to be left alone!"

Hurt flashed across his face as he stared at her, then he nodded, turned around, and finally left her bedroom.

She suspected he wouldn't be back, and strangely the thought didn't make her sad.

Instead she felt relief.

# CHAPTER EIGHT

Ethan crouched down behind his couch, one hand on his gun, his other hand closed except for his index finger, moving to his lips, signaling silence.

Beside him, his daughter nodded and pressed her back up against the back of the couch.

An obnoxious beeping noise sounded from across the room and Alison's eyes widened. Then, producing a blue and silver walkie-talkie from her side pocket, she pushed the button, making its own loud beep, and stage-whispered, "Are you in position?"

"Yep," the boy on the other end said simply.

"Agent Gru, can you see the suspect?" she asked Ethan.

Stealthily leaning around the edge of the couch, he stayed there for a few seconds before dramatically jumping back behind the couch.

"I've got eyes on the suspect," he verified, his voice dropping gravelly low. "He almost spotted me."

Her eyes went wide with an exaggerated look of horror. "We'll have to be more careful."

He nodded his agreement, extracting a little green disc from his pocket and sliding it into his colorful weapon. Then he pulled back the neon chamber and angled his Nerf gun upward. "I'm ready when you are, Agent Jessie."

Nodding solemnly, she said, "You go first, I'm right behind you."

Creeping up to the edge once more, he glanced back at Alison, giving her a nod, then jumped out from behind the couch, aimed his Nerf gun, and shot the little disc at the empty diaper box across the room, a dastardly face drawn on a piece of computer paper and taped to the front.

The little disc, unsurprisingly, did not knock the box over.

The little boy on the other side of the room "tackled" the box, and "Agent Jessie" went charging over there, her plastic hand cuffs at the ready.

To the side of the box, a row of 6 Barbie and Ken dolls were seated, piles of play money in their laps.

"You're not robbing these nice people today, Dirty Dan," his daughter stated, holding her handcuffs up victoriously. "Where's your accomplish?"

"Accomplice," Ethan corrected, chuckling lightly.

"I see her!" her playmate said, pointing at the giant My Size Barbie doll propped up against the opposite side of the couch.

"Dirty Debbie!" Alison exclaimed, running over to the doll, and calling back to the boy to "contain the witness."

"Detain...never mind," Ethan said, letting it go.

Alison was slapping the cuffs on Barbie, who of course smiled unapologetically.

Ethan made his way over to retrieve the little green disc before that one got lost like the other one had. They were little and plastic, but they still packed a punch, so the kids weren't allowed to play with them unless they were being closely supervised.

The little boy, ready to move on since they busted the criminal, jumped up and down and said, "Now what should we play?"

"I still want to play cops," Alison stated.

"Okay. But not another bank robber. What else should we do?"

Alison brightened and ran over to grab her My Size Barbie. "I know! Let's rescue this girl, she got kidnapped like those little girls you saved, Daddy."

Feeling the color drain from his face as his daughter thrust the giant doll at him, he couldn't even respond.

"Here, you hide her, you can be the bad guy, and we'll come find her and arrest you."

"No," he said, averting his eyes and putting his hand up to cover the doll's face.

A lump sprung up in his throat unexpectedly, and he knew playtime was over.

Alison frowned up at him, her little mouth turned down unhappily.

"Why don't you guys go get a snack," he suggested. "Your mom's in the kitchen."

"She's making dinner, she's not gonna let us have a snack," Alison said.

"Just... I have to go in my office," he said with less patience than he intended. "Go see your mother."

The furrowing of her little brow deepened and she gave him her angriest pout. When it achieved nothing, she sighed loudly and stomped over to put Barbie on the couch, then she said, "Come on, Braden."

"But I thought we were gonna play," he whined.

"My dad said no," she said accusingly.

Ethan sighed, closed his eyes, and passed a hand over his face, swearing under his breath.

Since it was the only place he could retreat to without leaving the house, Ethan hid out in his study, closing and locking the door behind him.

Collapsing into his big leather chair, he let his head fall back, closing his eyes and letting out a world-weary sigh.

A minute later he touched the mouse, moving it to wake his computer monitor up and leaning forward to type in his password. Once everything was loaded and his desktop popped up, he stared at the black screen—it used to be a picture of Amanda and the kids, but ever since he got back, he found the picture too distracting. Too depressing. A nice black screen didn't judge him.

He navigated to his bookmarks—he had the fucking page bookmarked—and located the folder and page that he wanted.

A moment later, the news story loaded with the picture of the girl sitting on a picnic table, a blue binder and her cell phone beside her, a big smile on her beautiful face, her gray eyes clear, happy, everything a 17-year-old's should be. She wore a denim mini-skirt with a blue and black V-neck top (which several dickheaded commenters had some fun with— obviously the only way the putrid little pissants could feel good about themselves) and she looked so…young. Not child-like by any means, but still…young.

He didn't know why he kept looking at her goddamn picture. It wasn't like he needed visual reminders; he thought about it all the time. Thought about *her* all the time. Wondered how she was coping, if her life was returning to some state of normalcy, hoping that she didn't see the same news stories he'd seen.

It wasn't uncommon for him to check out her social media accounts when he had a spare minute, just to see if there was any indication, but she had no online presence whatsoever. Since she had updated them once every day or two before the kidnapping, he took that to mean she was still in a bad place. Even her friends had stopped leaving her comments, and just the night before, he noticed the boy who had been listed as her boyfriend no longer had a visible relationship status, though Willow's still said she was in a relationship. Whether or not that meant anything, he didn't know.

It wouldn't surprise him if the relationship had crumbled. She was a teenager in a relationship with another teenager trying to cope with everything; he was a grown-ass man in a long-term relationship with his wife, the mother of his children, and he could barely keep his own relationship afloat after everything that had happened.

Amanda was a patient woman, or else he would already be in the dog house.

Finally he took one last look at the happy girl in the picture and closed the window, leaning back once more, still feeling restless.

The little black corded phone on his desk caught his attention. For no good reason that he could come up with. He had a separate line in his office, obviously, since he needed privacy for the business-related calls he made.

Over the years he had successfully reunited so many missing girls with their families, helped put an end to the horror they were facing—those that had actually been kidnapped, and a couple of times, even those who hadn't, but weren't as street-smart as they thought they were—and it felt like all the good he had done was wiped clear by the one unforgivable instance where he had harmed instead of helped.

For a few minutes, he took turns alternately staring at the phone and staring out the window. He needed to get it together. Get the girl off his mind so he could go have dinner with his family and pretend to be a normal person.

Instead of doing that, before he could talk himself out of it, he grabbed his phone off the desk, set it down in his lap, and dialed the girl's number.

His heart pounded faster; he knew he was making a mistake. He needed to leave her alone. It wasn't like he could ask her how she was doing.

After two rings, just before he was about to hang up, she picked up the phone.

"Hello," she answered, her voice light, normal, like he would expect any other 18-year-old girl's voice to sound.

He didn't say anything. He wished that he could tell more by her tone—how she was doing, if she was reasonably okay.

"Hello?" she said again, more forcefully that time.

He debated speaking—but only for a second. Quickly ruling that out, he hung the phone up.

Then he swore.

He shouldn't have done that.

That was stupid and insensitive.

Cursing again, he put the phone back on the desk and stood up, feeling more frustrated with himself than he had when he slunk into his office in the first place.

"Jesus Christ," he muttered, shaking his head and making his way around the desk and toward the door.

Then he felt a vibration coming from his left pocket. Pulling his phone out, he glanced at the caller ID…and nearly had a heart attack.

It was Willow's cell number.

Heart plummeting, he debated not answering it. She couldn't have known it was him—he had called from a blocked number. Preparing to apologize anyway, he answered the phone and slowly put it to his ear.

"Hello," he said hesitantly.

"Hi," she said simply.

There were a few beats of silence while he waited for her to ask why he had called, even though he had no idea how she knew he did.

What did he say? Wrong number? That was stupid. How would he accidentally dial her number? That would be even worse, because then she would know he had it memorized and she'd think he was some psycho stalker.

Although he was sort of a professional stalker, so....

The girl cleared her throat. "Sorry. Um, I'm not sure why I'm calling."

"You're not?"

"No. Sorry. I'll just go."

"No, wait," he said with a little more energy. "It's okay. Did you need something?"

The line was silent and for a second, he thought she had already hung up.

"Willow?" he questioned.

He heard her sigh, so at least he knew she was still on the phone. "Do you ever have dreams about what happened?"

Absently glancing at the clock to make sure it *was* only 6 o'clock, he replied, "Yeah, I do. Sometimes."

"Me too," she said. "They're different sometimes though. Like, sometimes it doesn't happen the way it actually happened, and then when I wake up I'm not really sure how to feel."

Ethan made his way back to his computer chair, slowly sinking down into it. "Well...how do you mean?"

Another sigh. "I don't know. Are your dreams all memories or are they different sometimes?"

That was the last thing he wanted to willfully dredge up, but he doubted she was eager to either, and she was doing it. "They're different a lot of the time," he said.

"Like how?"

He got the feeling she was digging for a specific answer, and he was growing too uncomfortable to beat around the bush. "What do you mean, Willow?"

She was quiet for a second, then she said all at once, like she might chicken out if she didn't say it fast, "I mean, is it always—is it always rape?"

Jesus Christ.

He didn't realize he had said it aloud until she abruptly apologized and said she had to go.

"No, wait, Willow." Fuck. Roughly passing his hand over his mouth, he exhaled and then before he could think better of it, admitted, "No, not always."

The line went silent.

He pulled back the phone to see if she hung up, but she was still there.

He didn't prompt her that time. He wasn't sure he had given her the right answer, and if he did, he wasn't sure *how* it was the right answer. Logically he could only come up with one reason for her to ask that, and that was that she was having them, too. Whether that made his answer better or worse, he had no fucking clue.

She was quiet for another few seconds, then she said, "Yeah, same here. I thought that might be weird."

It might be, for all he knew, but he wasn't going to tell her that.

"Feel whatever you're feeling," he said instead. "Don't worry if it's weird or not."

"Is that what you're doing?"

His dark eyebrows shot upward, somehow surprised by that question. "No," he answered honestly. "But I'm not the victim here."

"I don't like that word," she stated.

"Sorry."

"I feel like…I keep pushing away everyone who loves me because I just want to be left alone, but when I'm alone…a lot of times I find myself thinking about you."

Since she had just described his daily routine exactly, he knew how she felt.

He *was* surprised that she was in the same place though. Her thoughts were probably a lot different than his.

"Really?" he asked.

"Yeah," she murmured. "I know, that's probably weird."

"Probably," he allowed, nodding even though she couldn't see it. "But I'm going through the same thing, so… I'm not really one to judge."

"Really? You think about me?"

The way she asked that made him second-guess his honesty.

Maybe he shouldn't be encouraging further contact. He had no idea how to help her and she was a young, fatherless girl in a fucked up situation. At the end of the day, despite their shared experience, he didn't *know* her.

Clearing his throat, he said, "I think about what happened, of course. Like I said, I have a daughter."

Another pause. "How old's your daughter?"

"Eight."

"How old are you?"

"Me? I'm 32. An old fogey," he added, in some ill-fated attempt at levity that only caused him to cringe at how stupid he sounded.

But she laughed. Just a little. "Nobody uses that word."

"See, that's how old I am," he joked.

"You must have been there when they assembled the Statue of Liberty."

"No, that was actually finished the week before I was born," he replied, surprised to feel himself smiling.

He heard her chuckle again, and his smile widened, turning into a bit of a grin.

"Does your wife know?"

Just like that, the smile was gone. "No. I couldn't..."

"I understand. I wouldn't have said anything either. Didn't," she amended. "My parents want me to go see a counselor."

"Maybe you should. It might feel good to have someone to open up to."

"Maybe. I haven't decided if I'll go or not."

"Well, for what it's worth, I think you should."

"I should probably listen to someone as old and wise as you, huh?"

Smiling again, he said, "Yeah, probably."

"What are you doing tonight?" she asked suddenly.

"What am I doing?" he reiterated dumbly. "Well, I'm about to go have dinner. What about you?"

"My family's taking me into the city to go to my favorite Italian restaurant. We were supposed to leave about ten minutes ago actually, but they won't dare rush me. If I wanted to go on a puppy-kicking spree they wouldn't say anything."

"Yeah, porcelain-doll syndrome."

"Is that a thing?"

"Not a real thing, but it should be. You could probably get away with murder right now and they would just help you hide the body. Not that I should give you any ideas," he said lightly.

"Nah, the people I would want to murder are all in jail right now anyway. Hopefully some hardened prisoner will shank 'em for me."

"Jesus," he said on a laugh.

"I'm sort of joking. Not really though. Fuck those guys."

"Indeed," he replied.

"Well… I should probably go before I make us lose our reservation. I'm on my cell, but… I can't exactly talk to you in the car with my whole family listening."

"Probably not a great plan," he acknowledged.

"Sorry if I kept you from your dinner."

"No, not at all," he assured her. "I was just sitting in my office anyway."

"Thanks for talking to me."

He wanted to thank her, too, but he couldn't put into words what for.

So instead he found himself saying, "Feel free to call anytime."

Which, obviously, was not the smartest thing to say.

"Okay," she said, after missing a beat. "Enjoy your dinner."

"Yeah, you too."

And then she hung up, without another word.

Ethan just sat there staring at his cell phone, unclear on what the hell had just happened.

For a minute, he just let himself absorb the fact that the phone call had actually happened, not even delving into the contents of it.

He felt oddly guilty, and he couldn't say exactly why.

The doorknob jiggled as someone tried to open it.

"Ethan?"

Of course, it was Amanda.

Weirdly, the guilt started to swell. He assured himself he hadn't done anything wrong—anything *new* anyway—but it was still there, in the pit of his stomach.

"I'm coming out," he called back. "Just finishing up some email."

"Well, you can do that later. Dinner's ready. Why'd you lock the door?"

He stood, and as he did he felt his cell phone vibrate again.

It was a text that time, and it was from Willow. "This is probably going to sound really weird, but did you call me a couple of minutes ago?"

Shoulders slumping forward, he closed his eyes, pinching the bridge of his nose.

"Ethan?" Amanda asked more sharply.

"Sorry, I'll be right out, I'm sending an email and then I'll be right there."

He wasn't sure if he should tell the truth or ignore the text altogether, but he didn't want to be mean, and he really didn't want to lie to her, either.

So before he could consider the possible ramifications of his answer, he typed back, "Yes. Sorry."

Half a minute passed, then she replied simply, "Don't be."

He went into his messages and deleted those texts, then he opened the call log and hesitated, wondering if she would call back. Maybe he should program her number into his phone under Bill or something... of course, he didn't know anyone named Bill, and due to the nature of his work he didn't program any numbers into his phone anyway, so that was probably a ridiculous idea.

Clearing the call log, he shoved the phone back into his pocket and told himself to stop acting like a shady asshole.

# CHAPTER NINE

Willow had no desire to go back to school.

It wasn't even because of what she had experienced over the summer; she had never really liked high school. It didn't help that everyone knew some version of what had happened to her though.

Mostly because of her own actions, she didn't have any girlfriends left to go school clothes shopping with. Briefly she thought about calling her old friend Kathy, who could always be relied on to want to go shopping, but the prospect of enduring the inevitably awkward phone call in order to achieve that was enough to put her off the idea.

So, for the first time since she was 13, she went school clothes shopping with her mom.

Frowning as she looked through the hangers of clothing Willow had handed her for the "yes pile," Lauren said, "Honey, don't you think these are a little…mature?"

Willow glanced over her shoulder at the bright chiffon blouse at the front of the pile. "What are you talking about?

That's totally bright and playful. I could pair it with a tight black mini-skirt and wear it out clubbing."

"Well, sure, but…I mean, do you think this is what you really want to wear to history class?"

Rolling her eyes but smiling slightly, Willow said, "I'm not taking any history classes, Mom."

"Everything you bought from that last store was very business-casual. Don't you want to go to that Abercrombie store?"

"Ugh, no. I wore crap like that last year—not Abercrombie, because ew, but…no. I want to try out a different style this year. Change it up a little."

"It just doesn't look like anything your friends would wear. It doesn't look like how a *high-schooler* should dress."

"I'm barely a high-schooler anymore," Willow pointed out.

Raising her eyebrows, Lauren said, "You have a *whole* year left, honey."

Sighing, Willow said, "Look, if you don't want to buy them for me, just say so. It's fine, I still have some birthday money, I'll just have to weed a few tops out."

"No, of course I want to buy them for you, I just… You look so grown up in all of this."

"Well, Mom, I *am* grown up."

Lauren held up her least favorite item, a black dress that zipped up like a hoodie. "I still think this is…I don't think you would even be able to wear this to school."

"I'll wear it on the weekend. It's super comfy."

"It's going to get cold soon, this isn't appropriate for fall or winter, this is practically a beach cover up."

"Mom."

Lauren sighed, but put the dress back in the yes pile.

"Ooh, what do you think of this one?" Willow asked, holding up a black bandage dress with a red gossamer bodice and peek-a-boo sleeves. "I think I should try this on."

"I think that looks very sexy," her mother said, in a way that made it clear that was not a compliment. "Don't take this the wrong way, but you aren't exactly going on a lot of dates, and—is that another zip-up dress? What is with all of these dresses that seem to be made primarily for being taken off?"

"I think it's beautiful," Willow stated. "It would be nice if I *did* go on a date."

At that, her mother perked up like a dog at the dinner table. "Do you have anyone in mind?"

"No," Willow stated firmly.

"Have you talked to Scott lately?"

Sighing heavily, Willow ignored the question. Her mother *loved* Scott, and was heartbroken when she discovered Willow had ended their relationship.

"I was talking to his mother the other day…"

Willow tuned her mother out as she recounted whatever inane conversation she had with Scott's mother and headed for the fitting room, her mom following along behind her, still talking.

Once inside, she tried on the dress—which was really tricky, since it *did* zip all the way up at the back. It required some creative movement to get the thing all fastened, but when she did, she grinned at her reflection in the mirror.

She looked beautiful.

And yes, sexy, but she was trying not to be afraid of that thought anymore.

Stepping outside so her mom could see her in the dress, she smiled hopefully, wanting her mom to see that the dress made her happy, so she might be more inclined to open her wallet for it.

A bit wistfully, her mom offered a sad smile. "You look like such a little adult in that dress."

Willow cracked a less charming smile and snorted. "A little adult? Mom, I'm 18, not 8. I *am* an adult."

"You shouldn't be in such a hurry to grow up. It's not all it's cracked up to be, I promise."

Rolling her eyes, Willow said, "Mom, stop. I'm 18 years old, and growing up is not optional."

"Why don't we just go back to the preppy stores and get you some ripped jeans and sweatshirts?" Lauren suggested.

"No, I want to wear these clothes."

"Will you at least wear pigtails with it?"

Cracking a smile, Willow said, "If it will make you feel better, I can totally rock the pigtails."

Lauren sighed and waited patiently while Willow stepped back into the dressing room to change. Before she did, on a whim, she snapped a picture of herself in her pretty dress, then she set about getting the dress off and her jeans and tank top back on.

By the time they left the mall, they had bags full of clothing that Lauren didn't fully approve of, but Willow was quite happy with the haul.

When her mom half-joked that her new wardrobe would scare off all the boys at her school, Willow barely stifled a mumbled, "Good."

High school guys were stupid anyway.

Her thoughts drifted off to the man who had unwittingly taken her virginity.

Well, not really to *him*, but more to the dream image of him that she still couldn't shake.

When she couldn't take any more of the bad dreams, constantly waking to a blanket of terror, she had tried to retrain herself, to think differently. Before she would go to bed, she would think of Ethan, since she knew he would be there when she closed her eyes anyway, but she thought of him differently. Instead of fearing the bad dreams, she would think of the odd good dream that he had been in, or the fairly nice phone call—the fact that he was probably a totally decent person in reality.

Plus, well, he was attractive.

And even if it made her feel weird at first, having some twisted version of a sex dream about him was a hell of a lot better than reliving being raped.

It wasn't even close.

She still had bad dreams sometimes—sometimes featuring the unpleasant loss of her virginity, other times just dreaming about that room she had slept in, the other girls, occasionally being kidnapped again. Once she dreamed about the dead woman with the gun—she was going to shoot Willow in the face, but she woke up before the bullet hit her.

Other times, she had dream-memories of watching the woman be shot, hunching down in the corner, convinced she was seconds away from being similarly slaughtered.

Those were unpleasant thoughts.

She had promised herself she wouldn't go there while she was out with her mom. When she was alone at night those thoughts usually reoccurred, but if she kept busy during the day, she found it easier to keep them at bay.

She could only keep so busy at night though.

Shoving those thoughts away, she opened up her phone to look at the picture she had taken in the dressing room. It was pretty good, as far as dressing room selfies went.

Since she couldn't even remember the last time she had posted an update, she decided to go ahead and post the picture, with the little caption, "School clothes shopping with my momma!"

It felt frivolous and silly even as she posted it, but within seconds, someone had already liked it.

Smiling slightly, she closed the app and prepared to put her phone away, but on second thought, she opened up her text messages.

Most of the recent ones were from her parents and her brother, Todd. Just below those, however, were the messages she hadn't gotten around to deleting, even though she figured she probably should. Her mothers certainly didn't seem the type to go snooping through her stuff, but on the off chance, she had saved Ethan's phone number into her contacts under the name Shelly. If they ever tried to play detective and snoop through her stuff, they wouldn't look twice at a text message from Shelly.

She was no good at remembering phone numbers. Plus, she was lazy about deleting things. There were thousands of messages in her email inbox for exactly that reason.

"Do you think you'll still be able to do once-a-week appointments when you're back in school?" Lauren asked suddenly.

Willow had started seeing the counselor the week after her phone call to Ethan. It wasn't helping all that much, however, since she still got pissed off when anyone wanted her to talk about the whole ordeal. She also refused to tell the counselor about Ethan. Ashlynn had assured her she could—and should—tell the counselor anything and everything, but Willow wouldn't.

It wasn't only because she didn't want to get him in trouble; she didn't want to acknowledge what he had done. It clashed with her new view of him, and she needed that to keep her sanity.

And a little because, despite Ashlynn's assurances otherwise, Willow couldn't shake the idea that the counselor would tell. If Ashlynn knew the truth, she would drive to Ethan's house and gut him before Willow could even attempt to explain the situation.

Not that she could blame her. If Willow had a daughter, she would feel the same way, but since she didn't, she didn't have to think about it from that angle.

That night Willow and Todd got roped into hanging out in the family room and watching some television after dinner. While her moms watched some dumb sitcom, Todd spent the whole time text messaging some girl he claimed not to like, and Willow spent some time playing around on her phone, noting that 70 people had liked the picture she posted earlier and scrolling through to see what was going on in the lives of her old friends.

There was a picture of Scott with some girl named Holly that Willow didn't recognize. The comments all alluded to a relationship, but his status hadn't changed, so she wasn't sure. It seemed like she should care more than she did.

She didn't think anyone noticed her snooping until Todd murmured, "He's an asshole."

Glancing up in surprise, she asked, "Who?"

He nodded toward her phone. "I saw that picture earlier."

"Oh." Willow shrugged. "It's okay, I dumped him anyway, not the other way around. It's high school, he's bound to date someone else and I'm bound to run into them in the halls. At least she's not one of my friends."

Calling them her friends seemed a little odd, but calling them her "old friends" felt weirder, so she went with that.

"Still," he put in loyally.

Willow offered him a little smile. "Who are you texting?"

"Nobody." He glanced up as she quirked a brow and he sighed, lowering his voice. "Becka."

"I thought you totally didn't like her," she said lightly.

"We're just friends."

"Does she know that?"

"I don't know, girls are dumb," he stated.

"Um, no, I'm pretty sure boys are dumb."

For the next few minutes they bickered back and forth like they used to and it was a nice change of pace. Willow didn't even realize the sitcom had ended and the news was on until Todd had to go back to texting Becka, who thought she was being ignored.

"That's just awful," Ashlynn was saying, shaking her head.

Willow glanced at the television to find out what Ashlynn was talking about and saw a news story about a 15-year-old girl who had been kidnapped and kept in some deranged man's basement for several months. He'd been captured and in addition to the kidnapping charges, he was being charged with rape, to the surprise of absolutely no one.

"I just can't handle stories like this anymore," Lauren stated.

"Rotting in jail isn't good enough for that monster," Ashlynn added.

Lauren shook her head, agreeing. "I'm just so glad you were rescued before anything like that could happen to you, honey. You were so lucky."

Ashlynn slid a glance in Willow's direction, catching the suddenly stormy expression on her face and reaching for the remote. "Well, I think that's enough news for one evening."

"I haven't seen the weather yet," Lauren objected.

"You can check it online," Ashlynn stated, changing the channel.

It was too late. Willow already felt the initial sinking sensation that slowly morphed into hollowness in the pit of her stomach. Lower in her gut, she was already beginning to feel a dull ache—the same overwhelmingly uncomfortable feeling that she got anytime she was reminded of her ordeal. Her therapist had given her some bullshit breathing exercise to do, but when feelings of anger and injustice were welling up inside of her, she wasn't thinking about breathing—and she wasn't about to start doing a breathing exercise in front of her family anyway.

The need to flee was coming on strong, like an itch she needed to scratch—but in her brain, where she couldn't get to it.

There was also nowhere to go. Out, away—anywhere, but she didn't feel safe by herself in the world anymore. Even though she was sure it was only her imagination, she still imagined people watching her, waiting for their next opportunity to hurt her.

A couple of times she even considered going to her father to see if he had any friends or associates or whatever who could just keep an eye on her when she had to go to and from school. She never went, afraid it would be too embarrassing, and he would probably just say he couldn't help her anyway.

She had started carrying a pocket knife in her purse, but realistically, she knew it wasn't likely to help her in the event that a few big men decided to kidnap her again.

Her own vulnerability was very discomfiting. She knew everyone thought she was fragile, which made her even angrier.

The only place she could escape the watchful eye of her family—while also not putting herself in actual danger, in her own mind—was her bedroom.

Pushing herself up off the floor, she made some mumbled excuse about needing to go put her clothes away and escaped up the stairs.

Once she was in her room, she found that she really *had* left her new clothes in the bags on her bed, so she sighed and started taking them out, folding them or hanging them and putting them away. The comfy black zip-up dress she kept out, deciding to change into it after her shower since she was only bumming around the house for rest of the evening.

Once everything was put away, she sat down with her journal—another thing her psychologist considered a good idea—and set out to write. Several minutes later, pen poised over the notebook paper, she hadn't written a single word. Considering she was still unwilling to write down what happened to her, she was unable to appropriately pinpoint why she was angry, and she settled for writing a bunch of synonyms for her feelings instead.

The exercise didn't lead to any real catharsis, so she finally abandoned the journal and went to take a shower. The giant spider crawling along the shower wall had other plans, so she spun on her heel and debated how long she would have to deal with Ashlynn's prying concern if she called her upstairs just to get rid of the spider.

Probably too long.

She didn't need a shower that badly.

Instead she changed into her dress and pulled her hair up into a heavy, messy bun on top of her head—her hair was getting too long for that particular style, and she was debating chopping some of it off—not even going to a hair salon, just going to get the scissors, going into the bathroom, and chopping it right off.

The spider occupied the bathroom, however, and the scissors were downstairs, so that plan was shelved.

Sighing as she crawled into bed, she kicked the notebook in the floor and curled up under blankets, staring out the window. It was still light outside—only a little after 6— and much too early to go to sleep. Plus she was all wound up, and going to sleep like that would be impossible.

Still, she had no more use for the day. Going to sleep and wasting her evening depressed her a little too, since it meant one day closer to having to go back to school.

Going to sleep was always risky anyway. Her method of trying to control her dreams wasn't infallible, and she wasn't in the right mindset at the moment. The more she went to bed in a negative or anxious mood, the more she would dream about all the really bad stuff. If she got in bed and tried to think about nothing, she would invariably become anxious about the possibility of having a bad dream—then she would. Kind of a self-fulfilling prophecy.

Since she was already in a bad mood, she attempted to color over the anger with nice thoughts. She was alive, that was something. She wasn't being forced to spread her legs for money multiple times a night—another boon. Resisting the memories of people dying right before her eyes, she went for super positive—the school year would be great! She would simply ignore what had happened and focus on her future.

Finishing high school and going to college would be nice. Maybe she would even meet someone eventually, someone to wear her pretty dresses on dates with, who would understand without having to talk about it that she had intimacy issues even she didn't understand, who would be patient—not even patient, because he wouldn't even care. Yeah, he would be so in sync with her that he wouldn't even need to discuss what happened or why she was the way she was. He would just *get it*—and accept it. He would accept every part of her. It wouldn't hurt if he was also nice to look at, tall, strong—into martial arts or something, so he could kick Tito's ass if she ever saw him again. Maybe he would even teach her, so she could kick Tito's ass herself. He would probably have dark hair, a strong jaw—definitely. Really nice eyes, a sexy smile.

She smiled faintly, closing her eyes. Yes, that would be nice. She would feel safer when he was around, and he would like her new, mature way of dressing. Somehow she might even find her way back to being able to think about sex without having terrible images flash across her mind—she could create new memories with him, and eventually it would just be a thing that happened to her in the past that she didn't need to think about anymore.

Then she remembered that "maturity" in even the oldest guys at her school wouldn't entail any of that.

Oh well, she would have to wait for college.

In the meantime, she would have to come up with a more realistic way of achieving those goals on her own.

# CHAPTER TEN

Sometime after daydreaming about scenarios in which she and her mystery college boyfriend—he was a junior or a senior by the time she fell asleep—would sit in coffee houses discussing life, philosophy and politics, Willow drifted off to sleep.

Suddenly the man named Chuck was standing in a dingy room, coaxing someone behind her. He reached over and pinched one of her breasts, causing Willow to cry out in pain, objection, humiliation. What was going to happen to her? She wasn't a fool; she knew that most of the other girls had been "broken in" by at least one of the thugs—but not her. They couldn't do that to *her*.

Then there was Ethan. Beautiful, terrible Ethan, unzipping his jeans as her heart pounded so loudly in her chest and her blood raced through her veins so rapidly that she could *hear* her body's reaction. She felt herself trembling. Heard her mind crying out in denial—it couldn't possibly happen to her, it couldn't. Someone would save her somehow.

But then he was behind her, smacking her on the ass, and tears were welling up in her eyes. She was helpless, out of control, at everybody else's mercy.

In front of them, the one called Lane spoke but his voice was her mother's as he said, "You're so lucky."

She wanted to lash out, to scream, to fight, but then there was a gun pressed up against her temple. She was crying, shaking—she didn't want to die. Not like that, not mostly naked in a dirty rathole surrounded by people she despised. People who didn't give a shit if she ever drew another breath.

Dropping to her knees, she held out hope that somehow she would be saved. She didn't know how, but she knew someone would save her—just like in the books or movies. The girl had to be saved—she didn't belong there. Things like that couldn't happen to her.

Except that it was happening. There was no hero to save her, only a room full of terrible people who placed no actual value on her life. People who probably wouldn't hesitate to kill her if she gave them even a flimsy reason.

Maybe if she got him off, it would be over. It wasn't like she had a choice anyway. She felt disgusting as she touched him, refusing to look above his waist—too humiliated to watch him as he watched her—if he was even watching her.

Then he was in her mouth, and she was crying, making a real mess of herself as she tasted him. It was impossible not to think about what she was doing to a perfect stranger, half naked, while other strangers watched.

Behind her, as she labored over a stranger's cock, she heard Lane/her mother say, "You're so lucky."

Waking with a gasp, it took Willow a moment to realize it had only been a dream. She wasn't really back in that awful place—she wasn't really being raped again. Only in her mind, like so many other nights.

Helpless tears welled up in her eyes, infuriating her.

She felt sick to her stomach. Her mind felt polluted— her sense of peace demolished. There was no healing. There was no getting better or moving past it. Nearly every night the same fucking shit—she experienced it over and over again. All the feelings were still there, even if it wasn't real, because it *was* real. It *had* happened. It wasn't just a bad dream.

To feel helpless was the worst kind of agony.

So she saturated her helplessness in fury—she deserved to be fucking furious. She had been wronged, her suffering did not spring forth from a vacuum—it was the result of her body and soul being violated, her ability to control what happened to her ripped away.

And for what? She didn't even know. She only knew that it wasn't right, it wasn't fair, and there wasn't a goddamn thing she could do about it.

Well, that wasn't entirely true.

Reaching for her cell phone, she lit it up, wincing at the brightness and impulsively going to her text messages.

She rolled her eyes at the name Shelly, deceptively posing as Ethan. Without bothering to check the time or consider his family, she rapidly typed out, "Tonight my mom told me how lucky I am that I wasn't raped while I was in captivity. I sure am fucking lucky!"

Well, it ended up saying she was "ducking" lucky because autocorrect was a prudish bastard, but he would get the gist.

"Fuck you," she said to her phone, throwing it down beside her on the bed.

Just lying there thinking about it, she could feel her face heating up, her rage building. She needed to release her anger, but that felt impossible.

Her phone vibrated and lit back up.

Picking it up, she read his message. "Are you okay?"

"No I'm not ok. I'm furious. I thought I was doing better."

He promptly replied, "Do you need to talk?"

"There's no one to talk to," she stated.

"I thought you were seeing a counselor?"

She couldn't remember if she had told him that or not, but she sent back, "Can't tell her."

She watched the screen for a minute, but it only dimmed and faded to black. He didn't seem to have a response to that one.

Dropping the phone back into the cushion of her blankets, she covered her face with her hands and tried to find her way back to a more peaceful mindset.

Her mind wasn't having it. The dream was too vivid, too real.

Then her phone went off.

She wasn't sure what she expected it to say, but she did not expect what she read. "Are you able to meet me somewhere?"

For a split second, she was so surprised that her fury was delayed, but then she remembered that she was afraid to go outside after dark, and even if she ran to her car, she would have to face the terror of running to it, then the terror of running back inside when she returned. It wasn't worth it.

"No," she sent back. Then she elaborated succinctly, "Afraid to go outside alone after dark."

The phone indicated he was typing, then he sent back, "Is your family asleep? I could pick you up."

She didn't respond. It surprised her, and she wasn't exactly sure how she felt about it.

Then he added, "Or I could just come to make sure you get to your car safely."

That made her feel a little bit better, but when she tried to imagine it, it still seemed scary.

She also wasn't sure seeing him would help… even if he was the only person who knew what happened to her, so he was also the only person who might understand why she still felt the way she did.

Finally, making a snap decision, she sent back, "Pick me up."

After he agreed and told her he would be on his way momentarily, she stayed in bed, pulling her blankets up to her chin. She had something new to think about, she just didn't know what to think *about* it.

Eventually Willow pulled herself out of bed to go into the bathroom and take her hair out of the messy bun, opting to wear it down in waves that fell all the way to her butt. Once more she considered the scissors, but it wasn't really the time for an impromptu haircut.

Even though she heard her mother's disapproving voice in her head telling her she should probably change out of the "beach cover-up" before she left, she didn't. She wasn't afraid to show leg; despite the fact that he was the one to hurt her in

the first place, she harbored no real fear that he would do it
again.

Her sometimes overwhelming distrust of *all* people and
things since she returned home occasionally tried to convince
her otherwise, but she thought his guilt was real. Ethan didn't
have sexually violent urges—he had just been in a bad
situation, exactly like she had been.

Until she fell asleep on another bad night. Then he'd do
it all over again, but it wasn't like her dreams were within his
control.

Maybe she should just stop sleeping. Too bad she
couldn't function without sleep.

Since she didn't want to get caught sneaking out—no
way could she explain that—she crept downstairs and didn't
turn on any lights. Her anxiety levels spiked—not only had
she refused to be alone outside of her bedroom since she'd
been taken, but she was essentially terrified of the dark, and
usually turned every light in the house on, even if she was just
going downstairs to get a drink while her family watched
television.

Sitting on the couch by herself in the dark, looking at
the door that strangers had walked through and then dragged
her unconscious body out of... wasn't exactly comforting.

Finally she saw a car pull up outside of her house, but she didn't unlock the door until he sent her a text to verify that he was there.

A split second later, her paranoia took over and she panicked—what if he was in on it? What if he *was* a bad guy posing as a good guy, and he had just been biding his time, waiting for his chance to take her back? For all she knew, he didn't even really have a wife or kids! She had seen no proof. Maybe he wasn't even Ethan Wilde. His picture probably wasn't listed on his website, since his job required anonymity.

She didn't unlock the door. She moved her hand away from the doorknob. Panic was rising up in her chest and she wondered frantically what she had done. Maybe she should go upstairs and lock herself in the bedroom with Ashlynn and Lauren and tell him to go away. If he didn't, she would know he was a bad guy and she could call the cops. Surely he hadn't brought anyone to help him, since he hadn't expected resistance.

"Are you coming out?"

Her heart skittered as she read the message. She was being crazy. Or had she been too trusting before? She didn't know, all she knew was that terror had wrapped its talons around her nerves and she was starting to shake.

"I changed my mind," she sent back, not sure what else to do.

"Do you want me to leave? Are you okay?" he replied.

"Are you alone?" she sent back.

There was a brief pause, then he said of course he was alone.

At first, she didn't know what to say or do, then she sent back, "Send me a picture of your driver's license, please."

"What?"

He was understandably confused—or was he reluctant, because he was really Jack?

A minute passed and then she received a picture message—Ethan Wilde, with his picture. Surely he wouldn't have thought to bring a fake ID, right?

She hesitated, debating trying to get more proof or assurances, but she began to realize that she was being crazy.

Shoulders slumping, still uncertain, she stared at the license for another moment, looking for anything that felt off, before she managed to get her hand back on the knob.

But she couldn't unlock it. The last time she had unlocked that door, someone had invaded her home and wrecked her life. She couldn't shake the fear that it was going to happen again—after all, why should she trust him?

Then she thought about the scenario at the pizza place, the girl who *had* been a spy…she was going to shoot Ethan.

There was no way they had the foresight to plan a long-con *that* long.

Instead of asking him to prove his identity again, she sent back simply, "Promise I'll be safe."

Without hesitation, he replied, "I promise."

It didn't reassure her like she hoped it would, but her memories of the night at that pizza parlor/whore house refuted her paranoia.

She unlocked the door and opened it, her body tense as she quickly looked out on her front porch.

Predictably, there was no team of goons waiting for her, only Ethan in his car, parked at the edge of her driveway. He had even driven up and turned around so that the passenger door was closer to her and she wouldn't have to walk all the way around the car.

Locking the door behind her, she sprinted down the steps and ran the length of the driveway, grabbing his door handle and throwing it open. Once she was inside, she slammed the door and said, "Go."

Nodding once, he switched the car out of park and started driving down the road.

He was quiet for a couple of minutes and so was she. Finally he asked why she had asked to see his ID, but once she got into the car with him, her sudden fears about him had leveled out and she was too embarrassed to tell him what she had been thinking.

"Where are we going?" she asked, instead of answering him.

"I'm not sure," he said. "Anywhere you want to go specifically?"

"Somewhere with lights. I don't want to be out here in the dark."

"Okay." He nodded briefly, but didn't say whether or not he knew where they should go. Willow didn't ask.

Several minutes later when Ethan pulled down a residential road into a housing development, she lifted her eyebrows in alarm. "We aren't going to your house, are we?"

A ghost of a smile flitted across his face. "No. There's a park up here with a well-lit basketball court and a clear view of the cars coming and going. I'm going to park there."

"Oh. Do you live near here?"

"Yes."

He didn't elaborate and she didn't ask him to.

When they got there, she felt a little more comfortable. He had been right about the basketball court; it was brightly lit, and the parking lot was right in front, so there was a lot of light spilling over, illuminating the area enough that she could clearly see Ethan—he was dressed in a maroon T-shirt and a pair of black jeans. She wondered briefly if he had changed, or if he had still been dressed.

It was after 11 by then, so he probably just pulled his clothes on before he left.

What had he told his wife? Maybe she was already asleep. If they had young children, they probably got up early.

That line of thought reminded her that she was standing in an empty parking lot with a full-grown man who was married with three children, and she was dreading going back to school.

She might feel a little more awkward about it if he hadn't also been inside of her, if she didn't have vivid memories of the man groaning as she took his cock into her mouth.

Shifting a little uncomfortably at the thought, she averted her gaze, focusing on the cement instead.

"So, what's going on?" he finally asked, shoving his hands into his pockets.

Willow looked up at him—caught him giving her a once-over, actually—and felt oddly defused. A half hour earlier, she wanted to rip his head off his shoulders, but something about his presence calmed her, made her feel not so alone.

"I…I was asleep, I had a bad dream and I wanted to lash out. I shouldn't have sent that message."

He didn't immediately respond. The silence made her uncomfortable so she stole a glance in his direction. He was also looking at the pavement, his expression pensive. "I'm not sure what to say here, Willow. I want to help you, I want you to…vent your frustrations, but I'm not sure how to bring that about."

"I know." After a few seconds, she said, "It's hardest at night. Too many shadows, I guess."

Ethan nodded as if he understood. "You weren't lucky," he suddenly said. "Your mom would never say that if she knew."

Her lips curved up ironically. "She might, actually. My mom… she doesn't handle negativity very well. She lives in denial. She would probably just say I was at least lucky I lived or wasn't passed around or that…you used a fucking condom. She would find the silver lining somewhere, and it would just piss me off even more. I'm kind of glad she doesn't know. I'm not sure I could handle that."

"What about your other mom—Ashlynn?"

Flicking her eyes in his direction, she said, "Ashlynn would castrate you. She was abused as a kid, so… she doesn't make excuses or look for a bright side."

"Noted," he remarked.

"Don't worry, I'm not going to tell her."

"I get the feeling she doesn't really trust me anyway."

Unable to argue with the truth, she nodded. "She doesn't really trust anyone with a penis. Plus… I shouldn't have been so weird around you at that awful dinner. That didn't help."

"It couldn't have been easy for you."

She choked on a bitter laugh. "Easy? No, none of this has been easy for me. I can't even climb into bed at night without being terrified of what's going to be there when I close my eyes. I was doing better for a while, I went 5 days without a bad dream, but then tonight… there was a news story about this kidnapped 15-year-old and then my mom… And that was all it took. Less than a minute of exposure wiped out any illusion of progress and it was just like being there all over again."

Her voice started to shake at the end so she stopped, turning and looking at the basketball court until she got herself under control.

"No, don't do that," he said, reaching out to touch her shoulder, intending to urge her to turn around.

She flinched, closing her eyes and tensing up. He immediately removed his hand and apologized.

"I meant… you don't have to hide it. That's why you're here, get it out."

"I don't want to," she said, shaking her head, still not turning around. "This was a mistake, I shouldn't have made you come out here. I don't even want to talk about it."

"Maybe you need to," he suggested. "Whether you want to or not."

Willow shook her head, but turned back around since she felt like she had her tear ducts under control. "What good will that do?"

His blue eyes widened slightly. "Are you serious? It could do a lot of good. It needs to come out. You can't keep your feelings bottled up inside, you'll only end up hurting yourself and you've been hurt enough."

There was a retort on the tip of her tongue but she shook her head, resisting. "It's not fair though. You're the only person I have to blame, and it wasn't even your fault. Do you have any idea how confusing that is?"

"Tell me," he implored.

She shook her head more vehemently. "It's too weird."

"Fuck weird," he said, surprising her. "Let me have it. Tell me I'm a bastard. I'm not gonna hold it against you."

Her eyes flew to his—she didn't like confrontation, but she kind of believed him. "How could you not? I mean… it isn't fair to you either. It's not fair to me because it happened and I have to live with it, but it isn't fair to…to yell at you as if you had a choice, as if you wanted to."

"The hell it isn't. I made a choice. I only had bad choices, but I still made a fucking choice. A nobler person might have died, but he would have died without raping you, without stealing your virginity."

Her face crumbled slightly at the words and he heard her breath hitch.

"Tell me what a fucking asshole I am, Willow. I can take it."

Swallowing hard, she turned away from him, not toward the court, just to the side, so she didn't have to look at him as he tried to pull the anger out of her.

He moved into her line of sight, raising an eyebrow expectantly.

"No," she said again, tentatively looking up at him. "I can't."

"Tell me, goddammit," he ordered, his voice lowering instead of rising, since that didn't seem to be working. When she continued to resist, he aimed a little lower. "Tell me about your dream."

That hit a little closer. He saw her eyes spark, her cheeks turn pink, her upper lip curl into an unintentional sneer that she caught immediately, pressing her lips together firmly but managing to hold her tongue.

He didn't want to push any harder than that, but he also wanted her to spill so she would feel better.

Ethan sighed, tilting his head back and peering up at the dark sky. "Come on, Willow."

When he looked back at her, he saw her hands were clenched into fists and he hoped that she was working herself up, pushing herself, because he didn't know how much more he could push without making matters worse.

"Was I in it?" he prodded.

"Yes," she ground out.

Progress—he noticed the rise and fall of her chest becoming more pronounced and he could see the resentment burning in her face.

He took one small step closer, swallowing the lump in his throat and threw all of his chips on the table. "What was I doing to you?" he asked lowly.

A breath escaped her like a hiss, her eyes met his furiously. Instead of answering that time, she flung herself at him, pulling her fists back and letting loose as she slammed them as hard as she could against his chest.

He hadn't been braced for it so he stumbled back a step, but managed to regain his balance and brace for another round.

The round didn't come. Instead when he looked at her, she turned away, her hands pressed against her mouth as she shook her head. "I'm sorry, I shouldn't have hit you."

"Yes, you should have," he stated. "Get it out."

"No. I…" She spun around to face him, her frustration clear. "I didn't mean to do that."

"I'm not going to stop you," he said simply.

Willow shook her head. "I just… It isn't fair. I don't want to feel this way, but then when I'm alone and I remember, I'm so angry."

"Tell me about it," he prompted gently, thinking maybe he had pushed far enough.

Still, she shook her damn head.

"I can handle it, Willow. You're angry? *Be* angry. Tell me. Show me. Hit me if it'll make you feel better, give me all you've got. I'm the one who hurt you, I'm the reason you feel like this, so fucking hit me."

"I'm not going to hit you."

"Why not?" He wanted her to let the anger out before it consumed her, turned against her. Once more, he took a step closer, squaring his shoulders and using his size to subtly remind her that he was more powerful than she was. "I hurt you, Willow. I raped you. I forced you—"

With something like a growl, she came at him again, slamming her hands against his chest, not just once that time, but repeatedly. He nearly lost his balance again, but managed to stay upright as she pounded her fists against his chest, emitting sounds of raw frustration with each strike.

She had more violence in her than he expected; he was definitely going to have bruises, but he let her keep going until she ran out of stamina, her breathing heavy and her eyes wet. He could feel her weakening with each swing, and she finally stopped altogether, her hands still on his chest, but her energy spent.

Not knowing what else to do, he wrapped an arm around her—only one so that she could get away from him if it was the wrong thing to do. Dissolving into tears, she wrapped her arms tightly around his waist and he tentatively brought his other arm around her, fully embracing her.

He didn't say anything else. Merely held her while she cried, hoping that it helped her at least in some small way.

After a few minutes, still with her face buried in his chest, she murmured, "I'm sorry...."

"Don't be," he said, lightly rubbing her back. Then, pulling back a couple inches, he added, "I want you to tell your counselor the truth. Tell her everything."

Glancing up at him uncertainly, she shook her head. "I can't. I don't want to get you in trouble."

"You won't," he stated. "Everything you tell her is safe, you're protected by confidentiality. The only thing she would be allowed to break confidentiality for is if you wanted to hurt yourself or someone else. You can tell her the truth, all of it, she can't tell anyone."

"I don't know...she would still know. What if she saw you somewhere?"

"That's not your problem," he told her. "I don't want you to keep all this anger inside. It isn't healthy, it's...poison. You'll never feel better that way."

Offering a watery smile, she said, "I feel better right now. Maybe we should just meet and I can beat you up every night."

Cracking a smile, he replied, "I think therapy might be healthier—for both of us."

She nodded, trying to wipe at the tears on her face with the shoulder of her dress, since she still had her arms wrapped around him.

Without thought, he reached down and brushed her tears away with the pad of his thumb.

The way she looked up at him when he did, all beautiful and vulnerable, her lips slightly parted, her face tilted up, basked in the moonlight... he realized he had made a mistake. The stirring in his groin and his slow realization that she was pressed up against his body, with only a thin layer of fabric between them verified it.

Her tongue peeked out, wetting her bottom lip, and he barely stifled a groan. He needed to let go. Loosen his grip, step back...hope that his growing arousal wasn't plainly visible.

For a split second, the wicked possibility of not letting her go crossed his mind as his gaze swept over her plump lips, her soft skin, the look in her eyes, the awareness of her breasts pressed up against his chest....

Before he did something else to regret, he released her and took a step back.

He wasn't sure if she actually looked a little disappointed, or it was his imagination.

Ethan cleared his throat awkwardly, hoping her gaze didn't drop as he shifted uncomfortably, attempting to accommodate his damn budding erection.

"I should probably take you home," he said lowly.

Willow could only nod, her eyes widening as she quickly made her way around to the passenger side and opened the door, sliding inside.

He sat in the driver's seat, a heavy ball of dread settling in his stomach. Should he say something? Should he ignore it? Maybe it was all in his head. Maybe she was just vulnerable, and he was just a fucking asshole who imagined an invitation that hadn't been there.

Jesus Christ.

As if she wasn't confused enough already.

When several minutes passed wordlessly, he glanced over at her and she glanced back. Then he turned his gaze back to the road, but since he had her attention, he said, "I'm sorry."

"For what?" she asked, a little cautiously.

Since he had more than one thing to be sorry for, and he didn't want to acknowledge the moment that just passed if she didn't, he said simply, "For *everything.*"

Willow nodded her head but didn't say a word. They spent the rest of the ride back to her house silent, each stewing in their own thoughts.

As he pulled to a stop outside her house, she opened up her purse and dug around until she found her house keys, then she hesitated. He thought she was probably afraid to go outside alone and he was just about to offer to walk her to her door when suddenly she turned and leaned over the center console, throwing her arms around him in a sideways hug.

"Thanks," she said simply.

Before he could think to respond—return the hug? Intentionally not return the hug?—she pulled back, flashed him a faint smile, and opened up the passenger door.

She hopped out of the car and sprinted to her front porch. He hated himself as he watched her dress ride up when she made her way up the steps.

"Jesus," he muttered, nonetheless watching her until she was safely inside her house.

Although he was still a bit dazed, he also didn't want to be castrated, so he pulled himself out of it long enough to put his car into drive and make his way down the road.

It was the longest ride home of his life.

# CHAPTER ELEVEN

He hadn't talked to Willow since that night at the park.

His curiosity was killing him. Was she pissed at him after she had recovered? Did she feel like he had tried to take advantage of her?

Since determining not to take advantage of her had caused many a cold shower, he thought it would be almost humorous if she did think that and she *was* pissed at him.

Almost, but not quite. He would feel terrible if she felt that way. He simply hadn't been prepared for anything like that moment. The dreams *he* had that night were X-rated, but they weren't memories or bad dreams, that was for sure.

She had been back in school for a little over two weeks, and he was curious as to how she was doing, but he felt weird about contacting her to find out. Instead, he checked her out online again. Her profile picture was still the picture of her wearing that damn tight dress that showed off her shoulders. He loved and hated the photograph—where most of the salivating males commenting only loved it.

Not that he could comment, obviously, but he could read the comments of the little shits who did and roll his eyes at them.

He hadn't checked her profile in a couple of days and he had some time in the office while he waited for a fax, so he found his way to her page, just to see if anything changed.

When he saw what had changed, he was floored.

Willow had been tagged in a status by some boy named Angel Rodriguez that read, "can't wait to take out my girl tonight," and had a fucking winking smiley face next to it!

His girl? Since when was Willow anyone's girl? That wasn't even the boyfriend she had broken up with, this was some new asshole.

Fax forgotten, he spent the next half hour investigating Angel Rodriguez and concluded he was not the kind of guy for Willow.

Not that he had any right to decide who her type of guy was...but someone needed to look out for her, right?

Willow was still listed as single, but he didn't even know if she would keep her information current.

He debated sending her a text message. Just a brief one to ask her how life was...let her know he was thinking about her?

No. No, that was stupid. He was only thinking about her because he knew she was vulnerable and he didn't want her to fall prey to any vultures that might be circling.

Like that Angel kid.

At the end of his stalking session, he concluded that he had no good reason to contact her and he should leave her alone, even if he did think that kid seemed shifty.

It was not his concern.

The fax came through, reminding him that he had actual work to do, and he put the girl out of his mind.

As it approached 9 pm, he was back in his office. He found his way over to the computer again, figuring he would just see if there were any updates. Strangely the first post about taking "his girl" out had disappeared from her page, but she was tagged in a new picture, and what he saw made his jaw go a little slack.

Willow was all sexed up. She had straightened her long brown hair, put on more make-up than she needed, but it enhanced her beauty and made her look older, and she was wearing a tight-ass black mini skirt with some flowy bright coral-orange shirt. Her legs looked fucking incredible, except for the hand resting on her hip—the hand of her date, Angel.

Ethan scowled. One look at the picture and he knew what was on that kid's mind.

His fingers itched to send her a text, but he stopped himself. He wasn't a fucking kid; he couldn't interrupt her date to warn her that the guy she was out with undoubtedly wanted to have sex with her.

She was also an attractive teenage girl, so she probably already knew that.

He still didn't like it.

What if *that* kid tried to take advantage of her vulnerable state? Teenage boys were little bastards, only thinking with the little head and certainly not mature enough to handle Willow.

What the hell was she doing?

None of his business, he reminded himself.

If Willow was moving on with her life, good for her.

Yep, good for her. She was probably capable of handling herself around a horny teenager—surely he wasn't the first she had dealt with.

But he was the first since losing her virginity.

Or having it ripped away from her.

By him.

He had absolutely no right to dictate who she shared her body with now that her virginity wasn't holding her back.

He told himself he was just worried about her well-being, but since the images in his mind were of her in that mini-skirt, and flashes of memory of the night he held her in his arms and she looked like she wanted to be kissed...he wasn't sure he was being honest with himself.

It didn't matter.

He was a married man and she was an 18-year-old girl.

It was *not* his concern.

---

As Angel accompanied her to her front door, shoving his keys in his pocket, Willow got the distinct impression that he wanted to come inside.

"Well, thanks for dinner," she said, offering him a smile as she stood with her back to the door.

"No problem," he said, grinning at her. "You looked great tonight."

"Thanks."

"I mean, you always look great," he amended.

"Thanks," she said, feeling a touch more awkward.

"We should do this again." He flashed her a smile.

"Yeah, we could probably do that."

Since the date had gone well—and it was their second, technically, even though she hadn't realized that hanging out in a group the first time had been a date—and she was agreeing to another one, it wasn't at all unreasonable when he leaned in to kiss her.

Quickly dodging him, she went in for a hug instead, and he seemed surprised.

When she pulled back, he looked a little less excited. Still, he assured her he would text her later, gave her another once-over in case she hadn't yet understood that he thought she looked good, and then finally turned to leave.

Willow opened the door and made her way inside quickly, locking the door behind her. Her stupid heels were killing her, so she happily kicked them off.

"So, how'd it go?"

Spinning around, she saw her mother in a robe, smiling at her.

"It was fine," Willow said briefly, heading for the kitchen to get a drink. "The food was kind of salty, so I need an IV of water, but other than that."

"Did you like him?"

Rolling her eyes as Lauren followed after her, Willow said, "Sure, Angel's pretty cool. He's funny, I like that."

"Are you going to see him again?"

"I don't know, Mom. I wouldn't start picking out the monogrammed bath towels just yet, okay?" she said lightly.

"It's nice to see you doing something normal again," Lauren remarked thoughtlessly.

Willow's mood drooped slightly, but she knew her mom meant no harm. Still, she quickly grabbed a bottle of water out of the fridge and told her mom she needed to go change into something more comfortable, then made sure to tell her good night, just in case she was expecting Willow to come back down and share more details.

Once she changed out of her clothing and into comfy pajamas, she flopped down on her bed and checked her phone. She went online to clear her notifications and saw a few new complimentary comments on the picture Angel had posted of them together. He looked more territorial in it than she was altogether comfortable with, and she didn't want him to go thinking they were a couple just because they went on— by *her* standards—one single date.

Her stupid ex posted some passive aggressive meme about a "whore" ex-girlfriend, which she suspected was aimed at her, but who really knew? When he passed her in the hall earlier that day, he had given her a pretty sour look, so it probably was. Seeing his bitchiness definitely made her regret dumping him though, so way to think that one through.

There was a new comment from one of her old friends that simply read, "deets!!!!!!! call me" which only served to enhance her annoyance with Angel.

Earlier in the day, he had posted a stupid status calling her "his girl" and he tagged her in it. As soon as she saw it, she removed the tag, lest everyone think she was in a new relationship, but since some of her friends lived on social media, she had not been quick enough.

"Stupid, stupid, stupid," she muttered to herself as she closed out the app and opened up her messages.

She had to scroll down to get to the last one she had gotten from Ethan.

Just thinking his name made her smile faintly, even though she was sure that wasn't the appropriate response at all. She hadn't even heard from him again after that night at the basketball court, so he was probably either weirded out by her, or he felt he had paid his penance by being her punching bag for the night.

Not that they talked regularly, but there had been a moment that night when she had actually thought he was going to kiss her—which was crazy, obviously, but she still figured she would hear from him after that.

It had effectively changed the tone of her dreams though. Since that night—when for a moment, he was just a handsome, mature guy who was consoling her in her time of need—her dreams about him were much more pleasant. Having sexual dreams about him prior to that had been weird for her—especially when she didn't know him at all. As she interacted with him more, the less awkward it became, and the less she cared if it was acceptable or not. No one else knew, and if it made everything easier on her, then nobody needed to have an opinion about it.

It might also be helping that she finally told her therapist the truth after he advised her to. The woman hadn't seemed surprised at all, and her expression remained stoic as Willow went on to explain the added complications and how Ethan wasn't actually a bad guy. By the end of her rambling, she wasn't sure what her therapist thought about it, because her face was so impassive, but Willow had an idea of how it must sound.

The only flicker of surprise she betrayed was when Willow said that Ethan was actually the one who told her she needed to come clean in therapy, followed by, "You're still in contact with this man?"

Still feeling like a tattletale in kindergarten, Willow went on another long-winded defense of Ethan's character and explained that she was the one who contacted him afterward. It was a close approximation of the truth, even if she left out all of the crucial details.

Although the therapist hadn't said anything about it— the session flew by—Willow felt incredibly defensive about Ethan. It felt like a little secret that was only for her, yet her more logical side recognized that the basis of their relationship was… well, a little warped.

Since she hadn't heard from him since that night, she also wasn't sure that their odd acquaintanceship even qualified as a relationship, but since she had rezoned him, she liked the idea that he was looking out for her. As absurd as it seemed, she even convinced herself that maybe he was why she had only been raped once. The other girls had all been used multiple times, generally by a couple different guys, except for one girl—Lane's favorite, who was solely "used" by him.

She wondered where that girl had ended up. In the bedroom she had been stuffed in, there had been eight to ten other girls depending on the night, but she only knew what happened to the ones at the pizza parlor.

Hopefully she was returned to wherever her home was—hopefully all of them had been.

Thinking about that brought her mood down a little, but she was surprised that when images of herself bent over in front of Ethan started to seep in, she was able to immediately shove them out and replace them with the night at the park, holding onto him as he wrapped his arms around her and let her cry on him.

That was a relief. Still an odd memory, but much better than the stomach ache that always accompanied the other ones.

On a whim, Willow checked the time and saw that it was still before 10, so she typed out a simple message to Ethan that she took his advice and told the therapist.

He responded right away, asking how that went.

"Can you talk right now?" she sent back.

A minute passed before he answered, "Not right this second. I'll call you in a few minutes?"

"Sure." After sending the message, she paused thoughtfully, then added, "Or we could meet somewhere. Whichever."

Another minute passed. "Are you hungry?"

Something like excitement spiked in her stomach, but she did her best to ignore it as she sent back, "I could eat."

"Do you like Chinese?"

"What a stupid question—who are these people who don't like Chinese and why are they in your life?"

"Good point," he replied, then told her to meet him at a Chinese restaurant she had never been to before that was apparently open until 10:30.

Hopping off the bed, she tugged her comfy top off and shimmied out of her pants, grabbing the skirt she had worn to dinner and pulling it on, then grabbing a little red cami top out of her drawer, and the black crochet—completely see-through—3/4 sleeve sweater out of her closet—it was casually sexy, and always fell off one of her shoulders. It was her favorite item of clothing before she went school clothes shopping.

Then she took the red suede ankle boots she had ordered out of the box—they were sexy as hell, but stiletto heels and they were not even remotely pleasant to walk in. Once she had pulled on her new outfit, she went into the bathroom to quickly spruce up her hair and make-up, and she was dragging lipstick across her bottom lip when she froze, remembering her mom was downstairs.

"Shit!" Throwing the lipstick down, she went back to her bedroom, opening the door and creeping out into the hall. The staircase looked dark—maybe her mom had followed her up. Creeping closer, she peered down into the dark hole that led to her living room.

The dark still creeped her out, so she quickly headed back to her room to grab her phone and purse, then proceeded to sneak out of her house.

# CHAPTER TWELVE

When Willow walked into the tiny restaurant, Ethan's last remaining doubt that agreeing to meet her was a bad idea evaporated.

When she flashed him a smile, he returned it and somehow managed to keep from ogling her.

Every time he saw the damn girl, she was dressed more and more provocatively. What the hell was that all about?

Reminding himself of her age didn't help. It should have, but it didn't.

The young man working behind the counter grinned widely as Willow approached, and greeted her with much more enthusiasm than he had greeted Ethan with.

"What are you getting?" she asked casually.

Ethan glanced over at her, attempting to keep his eyes on her face, but the temptation to look down at that damned see through shirt was very real. "Uh…I don't know. What about you?"

"I think I'm just going to get the teriyaki steak-on-a-stick appetizer."

"That's it?"

"Yeah, that's fine."

Looking at the menu, he suddenly didn't understand why he had picked a Chinese restaurant. Garlic and various other heavily scented sauces—he was not going to have fresh breath, to say the least.

"If I get fried rice, will you eat some?"

Nodding solemnly, she said, "You will never see the day that I turn down fried rice."

Finally going with sweet and sour chicken, they ordered their food and drinks, Ethan paid, and the smiling young man told them it would be a few minutes.

Ethan sat down on the red wooden bench against the wall and Willow walked over to join him, but apparently noticed that her boot had come untied. Seemingly without a qualm, she hiked her leg up on the bench beside him and leaned over that long leg of hers to tie it.

It was physically impossible to look away. Her smooth, toned leg was right there, inches away, and there was sexy on each side—sexy suede boots on her feet, an irrationally short skirt at the top. When he finally managed to force his gaze away from her legs to glance at her face, he thought he saw a hint of amusement there, just the slight curve of a smile.

She was doing it on purpose to torture him. She had to be. It was a genius punishment if that was her game. It also meant she trusted him enough that she wasn't afraid to tease him, which was somewhat reassuring.

She had been dressed the same way on her date earlier that night though, so maybe she just liked to dress provocatively. Effectively dulling his arousal, he considered that she might even be dressing like that *because* of what had happened to her at his hands.

He hoped not. As long as she had waited to have sex—and would have likely continued waiting—he imagined it wasn't something she would take lightly, and he didn't want to see her get hurt.

Knowing what shitheads teen guys could be—or really guys of any age, if he was being honest—he was afraid that would happen.

When she pulled her leg down and flashed him a smile before taking a seat, he cleared his throat and remarked, "You don't seem very hungry."

"Snack-hungry. I actually went out to dinner tonight, so…"

"You should have said something, we didn't have to come here."

"That's okay," she assured him. "Like I said, I love Chinese food. This is a great snack. What about you, miss dinner tonight?"

"Yeah, I had to work through dinner."

Her expression changed slightly as she nodded, looking less light-hearted than she had a few seconds earlier. "Ah. Saving more people?" She smiled, but it looked forced.

"No," he said. "The opposite, really. Potentially cheating spouse, so… more like destroying marriages."

Her expression lightened and she rolled her eyes. "You're a real-life superhero, you know that?"

A self-deprecating smile tugged at his lips. "Nah, I don't look good in tights."

"I'm sure you do," she returned with a playful smile.

Ethan quirked an eyebrow in response, but caught himself before he could toss back a response he would have to feel guilty about.

Deciding to get the conversation back on track, he allowed his eye to casually travel over her outfit. "So, you're awfully dolled up for a night in."

Glancing down at her outfit as if she hadn't noticed, she said, "Oh, this? Yeah, I wasn't at home tonight, I actually went out with a friend."

"Ah, a friend," he said with a nod, waiting to see if she would elaborate.

"Yep," she said.

Since she didn't, he prodded, "Girls' night out?"

Her cheeks flushed a little and she glanced down at her boots, absently kicking out at thin air. "No. Guy friend."

He knew that already—he also knew that wasn't what she wore—but instead of saying so he merely grinned and said, "Ah, you went on a date."

Her cheeks turned an even deeper shade of pink. "No. Yes. Maybe. I don't know, I guess."

Ethan nodded. "Did you have fun?"

"Um, yeah, it was okay." She took a breath and refused to look in his direction.

Letting it drop, he merely nodded.

A couple minutes later, their food was already done and since he preferred privacy—and the staff probably wanted to go home—they went out to his car to eat.

He expected her to be more finicky, but he was quickly learning that either Willow was getting comfortable around him, or she wasn't a shy person at all. While they ate, she boldly stole a piece of his sweet and sour chicken and shared rice from the same dish he was eating out of.

As she reached over and cut off another end of his chicken and popped it into her mouth, he glanced at her in amusement. "Not a germaphobe, huh?"

Raising an eyebrow curiously, she murmured, "Hm?"

He indicated their shared dishes. "My wife and I have been married for years, she still won't eat off my plate."

Willow shrugged, apparently unconcerned. "That's illogical."

"I mean, you say that now, but when you get mono…"

Rolling her eyes, Willow said, "I've had your dick in my mouth, I'm not going to get precious about sharing rice."

Choking on the Coke he had just taken a sip of, Ethan could only stare at her, eyes wide in surprise.

Willow merely shrugged and took another bite.

"Damn, Willow."

"Well," she said expectantly, her eyebrows rising. "Just saying."

He cleared his throat a couple of times, but he wasn't sure where to go from there. It was a damned unique situation.

"What did your therapist—er, how did that go?"

Twisting the lid off her Diet Coke, she took a drink and then screwed the lid back on, remarking, "It was weird for me, but she didn't seem surprised. Which I guess makes sense. A girl gets kidnapped and sold to a whorehouse, it's more surprising if she *didn't* get violated along the way. I explained the situation though. I mean, I know you don't know her or anything, but I wanted her to understand how it happened."

Ethan was glad that she finally told someone, even if it made him feel awkward to have someone else in the universe know what he had done. While he also wanted to ask more questions in his own self-interest, he also didn't want to pressure her to reveal any details about her counseling session.

"You know what actually surprised her? That we're still in contact. I wasn't sure if I should even tell her that, but since you said to tell her everything…"

Nodding, he said, "Well, I can see why that would be surprising."

"Yeah," she said, but her expression was non-committal. "I don't know. It sorta feels like you're the only one who really understands though, you know? My parents don't get it. Everybody else wants me to go back to the way I was before, but I don't think I can. Besides, I'm more interested in moving forward than back."

It struck him as a wise observation and he found himself nodding. Surprising himself with his honesty, he said, "I might be more like your parents than you think. I've been trying to find my way back, too, but I can't seem to get there."

Nodding as if she understood, she said, "Well, our circumstances are obviously different. It really hasn't been that long though, you know? I'm sure after a little more time has passed…it'll be easier for you."

"Maybe," he said, but didn't sound very convincing even to himself. "I'm afraid it's not possible to go back now. If I were a better or worse person, maybe, but I'm stuck somewhere in the middle."

Willow stared at him for a moment, then she said, "I forgive you, you know."

Even knowing she was trying to offer reassurance, hearing her say that only made him feel guiltier. "I hope you know you don't have to protect me," he stated, briefly meeting her gaze. "Whether or not you believe I acted with intent or under duress, it doesn't matter."

"I know that. I'm not worried about being a good person, Ethan," she added with a wry smile. "If I didn't feel like I should forgive you, I wouldn't. I'm not really the 'forgive and forget' type." Lifting her gaze to his, she narrowed her eyes just slightly, as if studying him. "I feel like... and this may sound completely crazy and I could be totally off-base, but I feel like maybe we're the same in that regard."

Frowning lightly, he asked, "How do you mean?"

"Well, you said it yourself, if you were a better person you would have taken a moral stand and refused to do it, even if it meant dying for your convictions. If you were a worse person, you wouldn't be beating yourself up about it so much and you could just resume your life. We're not good or bad, either one of us, we're just straddling a line down the middle."

He thought about it for a few seconds. "I can see your point about me, but I haven't witnessed anything in you to convince me you're not more or less good."

Without looking at him, she smiled very slightly as she put her teriyaki beef back into the container. "I'm here right now, aren't I?"

For a split second, his blood seemed to freeze in his veins. Unsure of what she meant by that, he regarded her semi-cautiously. "You needed someone to talk to."

"Mm hmm," she agreed with a nod. "And of all people, I reached out to you. I'm clearly a little more fucked up than you want to give me credit for."

He had no intention to ask, despite his curiosity, but somehow when he opened his mouth, the words came spilling out. "Why were you a virgin?"

Cracking a half-ass smile, she shrugged as if it mattered less than it did. "I hadn't met anyone I wanted to sleep with."

"At 18?" he questioned.

"Is that so shocking?" she replied, lifting her eyebrows.

Immediately conciliatory, he said, "Sorry, I wasn't trying to make you…self-conscious or anything."

At that, she actually laughed. "I'm not self-conscious. Why would I be? I'm not—" She paused, her amusement fading a little. "I *wasn't* a virgin because I'm a troll. I've had offers, I just wasn't interested. I don't find it in any way embarrassing to have standards, and having sex isn't much of an accomplishment. I know, I know, I'm a teenager so I'm supposed to be a wild, wanton creature, spreading my legs for any football player who smiles at me." She rolled her eyes, shaking her head.

"I didn't say *that*. I just wondered about it. I wasn't trying to say you're abnormal for *not* having sex, it just... I mean, you're an attractive young lady, so I wouldn't have expected it."

"I could look like an English bulldog and still get laid," she pointed out. "I'm a girl."

Biting back a smile, he nodded. "That's a great point."

Willow nodded. "I take it you were not a virgin at 18?"

"I was not," he verified.

"How old were you?"

"When I lost my virginity?" He laughed a little. "God. Well, I guess I was 16. My girlfriend at the time was also a virgin and she had high expectations for the first time—romantic dinner, probably some bullshit violinist going around to the tables, a hotel room full of rose petals and enough candles to light up the whole street."

"I take it that is not what happened?" she asked with a smile.

Ethan shook his head, eyes dancing in amusement. "We had dinner at this crowded Italian restaurant on Valentine's Day and I gave her a pair of earrings, then when we left she wanted to park somewhere to give me *my* present, and we had sex in the back seat of the car."

Grinning, Willow said, "She just didn't know what to buy you."

"A minute and a half of pleasure," he joked.

"Priceless!"

"Exactly." He was still smiling, shaking his head at the absurdity. "Ugh, it was terrible."

"From what I hear, the first time usually is. Especially if you were both virgins."

"Fumbling around in the dark is a real thing," he verified.

"Had you been together long?"

"Not really. We got together around Thanksgiving, so about three months."

"Were you together for long after?"

"Until June, I think. Actually, after we broke up she started dating a girl, so my buddies had a great time with that one."

"Aw," Willow said, chuckling a little. "You turned her off men altogether."

Shrugging good-naturedly, he said, "We're bastards, she was better off."

"That is true," Willow agreed with mock-solemnity. "My mom—my birth mom, anyway—dated men all her life until after she had me, but she said it always felt wrong. I'm sure your girlfriend was just trying to convince herself she was straight by being with you."

"I think she was bi, actually. She was with another guy after that relationship ended, but you know how guys are. Never lived it down."

"Yeah, guys can be pretty dumb," she agreed with a roll of her eyes.

He nodded. "Your brother—was he Ashlynn's biologically?"

Willow nodded. "Sperm bank. Ashlynn never slept with a man, to my knowledge."

"What about you? Did you—do you date a lot?"

"I wouldn't say a lot. The problem is sometimes I just want to hang out with a guy and not have it be a whole thing, but then next thing I know he's calling me his girlfriend or getting all mad at me for hanging out with some other guy— but I just thought we were friends, I didn't even realize we were dating. If *I* think I'm single, you can't be pissy if I go out with someone else. Make your position clear, dammit. That's the problem, high school guys are just…they're not bold enough, you know? They don't really know who they are yet, they're not decisive, they're too casual, they don't let you know where you stand, and God forbid you *ask*, because then you're a psycho-bitch. They're just stupid. I don't think teen guys are built for relationships, they're just wired for screwing around with their douchey friends and not taking girls seriously. I have not felt like any guy I've ever gone out with could really handle me."

Quirking a smile, he remembered thinking just that. He wasn't stupid enough to admit that, though. "You don't seem that high-maintenance to me."

"I don't think I am, I just think I'm going to have to hold out for college. I've always liked guys a bit older anyway."

"I'm shocked," he said dryly.

"I'll probably end up having an affair with a professor," she joked.

"I can actually see that," he replied, shaking his head. "You'll walk into class in that skirt and those boots and he'll just fall at your feet."

Grinning at him, she said, "You like my skirt and my boots, huh?"

"I am a straight man with a pulse, so yes."

She looked inordinately pleased. "I like them, too."

"I'm sure your date enjoyed them as well," he remarked, even though he knew she had changed clothes—for him, apparently.

Without feigning modesty, Willow nodded her head. "He is also a straight male with a pulse. But like I said, high school guys aren't that hard to impress."

Going for casual, he asked, "You think you'll see him again?"

"We're friends, so I'm sure we'll hang out again. Hopefully I won't find out Monday at school we're engaged, but you never know," she added lightly.

Ethan merely shook his head. "Sounds like quite the problem. I feel really bad for you. I'm sure being desirable is quite a burden."

Raising her eyebrows, she said, "Hey, it can be. You would be surprised how many guys see a reasonably attractive girl in a mini-skirt and make inaccurate assumptions about her." Then, rolling her eyes, she added, "And don't even start; you're hardly Quasimodo yourself."

"I'm retired from that whole scene. I can't say that I miss it. Dating can be the worst."

Willow nodded her agreement and then took another drink of her Diet Coke. "Luckily I can just avoid it until I meet my professor."

"Sounds like a plan," he agreed. "At least aim for an unmarried one under 60."

"Well, yeah," she said, rolling her eyes. "Mid-thirties is probably the cut-off. I prefer not to date grandfathers before I'm legally able to drink."

"Good God, you're not even legally able to drink," he said, shaking his head in bewilderment. "It's probably past your bedtime, you shouldn't even be here."

Leveling a dry look in his direction, she said, "Okay, let's not get carried away."

"You know, you really don't look 18," he said, somewhat accusingly as his gaze swept her outfit briefly.

"Age is just a number," she shot back cheekily.

Ethan merely shook his head. "I think your professor is going to be one lucky bastard."

She winked. "I'll tell him you said so."

A moment passed and Ethan closed the unfinished container of Chinese food. It occurred to him that he probably shouldn't take it home, since Amanda would wonder why he had gone out for Chinese food all by himself, and why he had ordered so much.

"So, sex in the backseat—that's probably not very comfortable, huh?"

Ethan's eyes widened. "What?"

She indicated the back seat with her thumb. "You said you lost your virginity in the backseat. Obviously I've never done that, but I always figured it would probably be pretty uncomfortable."

"Oh." It took him a few seconds to recover, then he said, "It can be. Depends on your position. I don't think we should be talking about this."

"We talked about it before," she reminded him.

"Well, yeah... but that was different. I was just telling a story, not..."

Willow waited for him to elaborate, but words failed him. She flashed him a little smile. "I was just curious. I wasn't suggesting we try it."

"I know," he said, wincing a little when he heard how defensive he sounded. Realizing how far off course they had gone, he attempted to lead them back. "Anyway, we were out here to talk about your counseling, not my sex life."

"As if there's no overlap," she remarked, but before he could even absorb it, she said, "I like this better. It's nice to feel normal for a night."

"This is normal to you?" he asked, his disbelief clear. "This is not normal to me."

Willow closed the container with her remaining teriyaki beef, sensing their time was nearing its end. "I'm trying to reestablish normal. That's why I'm trying to go on dates and stuff, but it's hard because for me it's just practice, but for them it's real. I'm trying to regain control over certain aspects of myself, but I have no control over other people. I need a guinea pig, but when I go out with some hapless guy, it's just like I'm using him or teasing him. I guess I don't really know how to explain it."

"You need a guinea pig in what way? To ease back into dating?"

"To ease back into everything. To…find my own sexuality again. To reaffirm that I don't have to be afraid, that guys are going to respect my limits and my wants and my desires no matter what, but that isn't *true* so how can I prove it to myself? I mean, it's not the same—it's not like my date's likely to force me, but they still want more than I want to give and then I feel guilty. I want…to call the shots, just so I know I can. I don't know how to explain what I mean without sounding stupid."

"You don't sound stupid," he said softly. For a moment, he was quiet, then he said, "I don't want you to end up in a bad situation though. Obviously your partner should respect your limits, but…"

He trailed off, looking for the right words, but failing to find them.

Willow didn't need the words. She nodded. "That's the problem. If a guy feels like I led him on, he could get pushy, and my luck I would find the one who *would* rape me, and then I would never trust another man ever again. The point is to prove that I can say no and a man who finds me sexually attractive will listen no matter what, not wind up in a situation where I actually have to say it and then he *doesn't* listen."

Upon reflection, that better explained the outfit she was wearing out to meet him. Since the horny high schoolers she knew clearly didn't make her feel safe, she was branching out, spreading the temptation around a bit. She did want him to find her attractive, but only to prove a point.

"If it helps, I find you sexually attractive and I've been able to control myself."

Willow smiled slightly. "Well, sure, but I also haven't tempted you."

"What do you call that skirt?" he replied, raising an eyebrow.

The girl actually scoffed. "You think showing a little leg is my best effort to inspire lust in a man? I think you underestimate me."

"Well...and the boots. Back at the restaurant—you weren't trying to get a rise out of me?"

Shrugging unapologetically, she said, "I was curious if I could. I wasn't exactly worried about you pouncing on me in the middle of a public restaurant either."

"I would never willingly pounce on you if you didn't want me to. I mean—you know what I mean. Obviously...circumstances being what they are... But if circumstances were different and… Regardless of the provocation, I would never ignore your right to refuse me."

"No matter what?"

"Of course not."

"If I stripped naked right in front of you and did the most erotic things you could possibly think of and you were turned on to the point of physical *pain*, but I was reluctant…?"

"I would remain in physical pain and not lay a single finger on you."

Smiling a bit wickedly, she said, "What if I let you put a finger on me? But only a finger."

The mental image she was creating for him was actually starting to rouse his fantasies, and he did his best to lock them down before he *did* become aroused like an asshole. "Same thing," he murmured. "If a man is worth your time, he will respect your boundaries and not move faster than you want to—no matter what."

"Maybe you should be my guinea pig," she suggested half-jokingly. "You don't expect me to fuck you, but you find me attractive enough that you want to."

Just hearing her *say* that caused his cock to stir.

In a sense, he agreed with her logic. If she felt the need to be provocative, at least he could be sure no harm would come to her at his hands.

On the other hand, that absolutely was not an option.

"At least, I think you do," she added when he didn't respond, her face turning pink.

"I do," he said brusquely. "I mean… I shouldn't say that to you, but it also wouldn't be a very convincing lie, all things considered."

Willow nodded her head, absently tracing shapes on top of the food container. "I'm making you uncomfortable. Sorry."

"No, I'm not…" Sighing, he thought about the 'discomfort' he had caused her, and how somehow she was still considerate of his feelings. "I suppose in a sense… it would be no different than going to a strip club, right? I mean, sex isn't on the table, so…"

Her eyes widened a little—clearly even she didn't expect him to even entertain the possibility. "I… right, yeah, I guess you could say that. I mean, I was just…honestly, it's just a theory, I can't even say for sure it would work."

Ethan was quiet for a moment, then he said, "It's your call. If you want to push the limits with someone in a safe environment…there's no risk with me. I can prove what you need proven."

Eyeing him up, Willow seemed to consider. "You wouldn't think less of me?"

"Of course not."

"Could we still be friends after, or do you think it would ruin it?"

Smiling a little at her naiveté, he assured her, "Yes, we could still be friends."

For just a few seconds, his mind filled up with all of the things he could teach her about her sexuality, about the uncomplicated pleasure of sex… but of course he couldn't, and even as a single man in his predicament, he wasn't sure sex could ever be uncomplicated between them given the horror of her first experience and his role in it.

Emerging from the stirrings of those less than platonic daydreams, Ethan frowned slightly as she put her food in the floor.

Then she said, "Shall we move to the back seat?"

# CHAPTER THIRTEEN

"I'm going to need a drink."

Willow's smile faded just a little. "Um, won't that...I don't know, lessen your control?"

Ethan shook his head. "No, I'm not going to get shit-faced, I just need a shot."

Instead of going to a bar, Ethan stopped and bought a bottle of whiskey.

Willow hadn't actually thought he would agree to it—had never expected to suggest it!—so as she sat silently in the passenger seat, watching out the window as he pulled onto the road, her mind raced.

Could she change her mind already? It wouldn't prove much of anything, but she suddenly felt insecure. Ethan was a grown man, and she had never *tried* to seduce anyone before. What if she just looked stupid? What if it was incredibly awkward? What if it brought back memories that she didn't want to surface? What if—worst case scenario—he was wrong and he did lose control of himself? Reliving her horror in nightmares was bad enough, but reliving it physically and all because of her own stupid idea? Well, that would destroy her.

He probably thought she was so dumb.

He was probably just agreeing out of guilt.

Then he pulled into a hotel parking lot.

"Um…what are we doing here?" she inquired, shifting uncomfortably.

"If we're going to do this, we might as well do it right," he reasoned.

"We're not going to have sex though," she reminded him, alarmed.

"I know. This will be more comfortable. Plus, whatever it is you're planning, I really don't want to get caught in the backseat of my car with an open container *and* an 18-year-old girl. This will give us some privacy."

That was a good point. She hadn't even thought of getting caught.

"It's just pretend though," she insisted, more for herself than for him. "Just…a test."

"Of course." He glanced over at her. "If you're nervous, we don't have to do this."

It was the out she had just been considering, but suddenly having him offer it changed her mind. Shaking her head, she said, "No. I may never get a chance like this again and… I would be pretty horrified if during my next *actual* sexual encounter I have a panic attack or something. I want to do a test run. This was my idea."

Ethan nodded. "If you change your mind at any point, just say so."

Since Ethan obviously didn't want to be seen checking into a hotel room with her, he told her to stay in the car while he went inside and got a room.

While she understood the need for discretion, it also made her incredibly nervous to sit in the car by herself. She kept fidgeting with her hands and looking out the window. The parking lot was well-lit, but she still kept imagining some goons showing up outside the door and ripping it open, yanking her out of the car kicking and screaming, taking her away to her own personal hell—again.

One would think that having a father with an illegal criminal organization at his disposal might allow for some kind of security, but apparently that was not the case. It actually pissed her off how little he seemed to care that she had been abducted by bastards purely because she was related to him.

Absently checking her phone—as if he would call her that late, or at all—she saw that nothing had changed

Since her brain had the worst timing ever, it chose that moment to throw her back into the past, lying on a dingy mattress in the dark room, then that bastard coming in to get

179

her and hauling her out to the main room where she would eventually see Ethan for the first time. He was dressed like the other flunkies—his jeans were a little baggy, his t-shirt a size too big, his raven hair was a little mussed, a shadow along his jaw betraying the fact that he hadn't shaved recently. His eyes stood out though—alert, not foggy like the other guys, who were *always* high. Also, they were a striking shade of blue, which she might have appreciated if he hadn't been in the process of making her worst fears a reality.

Back in the present, she wondered, *Do I really want to do this?*

Then Ethan stepped through the doors and made his way back toward the car, and a rush of warmth washed over her. He looked so much different as himself. Less rugged— his hair wasn't messy, no hint of stubble on his jaw, and he was actually wearing a suit, which is what she usually saw him in, so she assumed he must dress that way for work. It made sense—it made him look more professional…and more delectable, since a man in a suit pretty much always looked good.

Still, her first impression of him was flitting around the edges of her memory and putting her slightly on edge. What would her emotional response be if she put herself in a similar situation all over again?

Then again, maybe it would be the same even if he was anyone else, and then she would have to explain her freak-out to whomever that happened to be—and she did *not* plan on sharing that event with anyone in the future, if she could help it.

Ethan approached the passenger door and opened it. "All right, we're good to go," he told her.

Nodding a bit anxiously, she put a foot out of the door and stood, watching him close the door behind her and following him to the hotel entrance two doors down.

"Should we move the car closer?" she asked.

It wasn't far, but since she was still constantly in fear of being attacked at night, even a couple of yards closer would make her feel better.

"Before we leave I'll pull the car closer," he assured her. She nodded, satisfied, and watched him open up the door and gesture for her to go inside.

Immediately upon entering the room, she felt intimidated. Red carpet covered the floor of the large unit, and along the center of the left wall was a *giant* bed with crisp white sheets and a red blanket folded up, draped across the bottom. More pointed than that, when she took another step forward, she looked to her left and saw a corner with mirrored walls behind a big Jacuzzi tub on a white raised dais.

It was a room for sex, not sleeping.

Ethan's hand moved to rest lightly on the small of her back and she jumped, not expecting it.

"Is that okay?" he asked, glancing at her face.

Nodding despite her uncertainty, she assured him it was.

The door closed behind them but she didn't move any closer to the bed. In front of the bed was a dresser constructed of cherry-veneered wood, a mid-size television on top of it. Beyond the bed, in front of another door—maybe a closet— was a big beige chair with a matching ottoman.

"Want to watch TV?" Ethan asked lightly.

It was just the right thing to say. Willow cracked a smile and turned toward him, shaking her head no. Then, without a word, she decided to dive right in.

Her hands went to the lapels of his jacket and she began to peel it off of him. Surprise flashed across his features, but he let her do it, helping when one of the sleeves got caught. Just in front of them, before the dresser, was a mini fridge with a microwave on top, and once it was off, Ethan discarded his jacket on top.

"I forgot the whiskey in the car," he murmured.

"You don't need the whiskey," she replied, her voice a little less steady than she intended. Maybe *she* needed the whiskey. This was no way to pretend-seduce a man.

Before he could respond or remark on her clear uncertainty, she reached for the hem of her black crochet sweater and pulled it over her head, tossing it in a heap on the floor in front of the fridge.

Ethan swallowed, his gaze moving down her body—slowly, in no hurry that time, not trying to hide it. The appreciation in his gaze made her feel more confident, and acting on instinct alone, she placed one hand on his chest and pushed him backward until he was pressed against the wall.

Both of his eyebrows lifted in surprise and she fought the urge to ask if that was okay—she wasn't going to ask permission. Once he was there, she wasn't altogether sure what to do with him, so she just moved closer until her body brushed against his. Leaning in, she nuzzled her face against his neck while her daring hand left his chest and dropped lower, caressing his growing erection.

Closing his eyes, he tilted his head back and barely stifled a groan. Bringing her other arm up to wind around his neck, she trailed her kisses up to his ear where she experimentally took the lobe lightly between her teeth and tugged. One of his free hands moved to her waist, tugging her a little closer, and as her pelvis pressed up against the evidence of his arousal, a little gasp of her own slipped out.

"Sorry," he said roughly, releasing her waist and dropping his hand to his side. "I forgot the rules for a second."

Biting back a small smile, she said, "Well, don't do that. It's kind of the whole point. But you can put your hand back if you want, you just surprised me."

He merely shook his head, his hands remaining at his sides.

Instead of resuming her exploration, she took a step back. "I'm going to run to the bathroom real quick, I'll be right back. You can… get comfortable," she said, gesturing to the expanse of the room.

"Maybe I should go get the whiskey," he suggested.

She flashed him a smile over her shoulder, then disappeared behind the door.

Without delay, Ethan opened the door and headed to the car.

# CHAPTER FOURTEEN

Ethan was in hell. He had to be.

He also had to be absolutely insane to have agreed to this to begin with.

After three generous gulps of whiskey, he put the bottle down on the nightstand between the bed and the Jacuzzi—then, looking at the Jacuzzi, he reconsidered and took one more gulp.

His phone was still in his pocket, so he took it out to make sure he hadn't missed any texts or phone calls. He even considered texting Amanda to let her know not to wait up. Guilt tore at him then, but he didn't want her to worry either. Before he could reconsider, he quickly sent a message to let her know he would be out late, and as soon as it sent, he turned the phone off and put it on the table beside the whiskey.

How had his life gotten so fucked up? Mere months ago there was no imaginable scenario that would have put him where he was, and yet… there he was.

Even though it was her idea to begin with, he wasn't even sure Willow was on board. He didn't know her well enough to know how she was going to feel about even a mock-seduction, since it was obviously going to involve very real touching and sexual arousal. It seemed from her comments like she was okay with it—or could at least rationalize it in some way—but he couldn't say whether or not that was a front.

He might also feel less like an asshole if part of him didn't *want* to be there. If he could actually say the only reason he had agreed was to reassure her that she could trust a man not to force her into something she didn't feel comfortable with, and no part of him just wanted to touch her again.

None of that was true, however. Willow intrigued him; he couldn't figure out all of her responses to him in particular, and she seemed to have such a different perspective from anyone else he knew. Perhaps it was her age, the resilience of youth, but he didn't remember being so pleasant or casual about his own bad experiences immediately after coming out of them. He only remembered being an angry bastard.

It took him much longer to get to a place even remotely like the one Willow had been in all night, and he didn't understand.

But it impressed the hell out of him.

The bathroom door eased open and he sat up a little straighter, his eyes jumping to the little entryway she would emerge from, but she didn't immediately come out.

Then she did, and the erection that had dissipated started to come back to life.

Her clothes had been discarded, and as she approached him, she wore nothing but a light pink bra and panty set—both lace. Her feet were bare, with maroon polish on her toes, somehow highlighting her age in his mind.

God help him, it did absolutely nothing to extinguish his interest.

Her breasts seemed fuller than he remembered them being, but she was probably wearing a push-up bra. Since she had such fair skin to begin with, the pale pink lace only served to enhance his awareness of her near nudity.

Not touching her was going to be absolute fucking hell.

Agreeing to such lunacy was a huge mistake.

Without a word, he reached for the whiskey and took one more swig.

Willow cracked a smile as she approached the bed—and him—and stopped when her legs were maybe an inch from brushing his knees.

Oh, God, up close was even worse. His fingers itched to reach out and touch her skin—it was smooth, he suddenly remembered, and then all the other thoughts were flooding back, the bad ones he had been able to brush off in recent weeks. His hand stung with the memory of smacking her on the ass, and he was consumed with the desire to pull her closer, grab that ass, and yank her into his lap.

Instead of fulfilling his momentary fantasy, he placed the whiskey bottle into her outstretched hand.

She took a much smaller drink than he had, made a face, stuck out her tongue, and put the whiskey back down.

"Gross. That's…that's gross."

"You've never had whiskey before?" he asked.

She shook her head, then she looked down at him, seeming to drink in the sight of him slowly. When she finished her perusal, she ran her fingers through his hair and said, "You can touch me if you want to."

Oh, how he wanted to.

Since he couldn't do anything about it though, he thought it probably wasn't a great idea.

Still, he didn't want her to feel self-conscious…and he really, really wanted to touch her.

Starting just below her breasts, his knuckles skimmed her sides, coming to settle on her hips. Slowly, so she could pull back if it wasn't okay, he drew her closer, spreading his legs so she could stand between them, then he bent and placed light kisses along her stomach. He felt her quiver, felt her breath quicken, and allowed one of his hands to brush the curve of her ass.

When she moaned faintly, his grip tightened, his fingers curling more possessively around her ass.

Touching was too much so he pulled back.

Then she looked at him, her face clouded with desire, and he only wanted to touch her more.

Clearing his throat, he said, "I think maybe I'll let you take the reins for a few minutes."

"Already?" she teased, a smile grazing her mouth—oh, that mouth. He remembered the feel of her mouth around his cock, and it shouldn't inspire any sort of lust given the circumstances, but it did.

He attempted a smile, but the effort fell short as he shifted in discomfort.

"I'm supposed to be driving you to the edge of reason, remember? Making you want me more than oxygen so I can tell you no," she said with relish, her eyes narrowing as her nose wrinkled up adorably.

He didn't know why it surprised him that she might be playful in the bedroom—it suited her—it just wasn't what he was used to.

Nope, couldn't think about what he was used to. Guilt was not welcome in that hotel room on that night. He had a job to do—and he couldn't exactly complain about it.

"You don't have to try very hard," he said dryly.

It was true—he was pretty sure if she could get him going while crying in a room full of onlookers, she wasn't going to have any trouble turning him on half-naked in a hotel room.

Her smile weakened a little. "Are you having second thoughts?"

Second thoughts? Try tenth and eleventh thoughts. Instead of being honest, he merely shook his head. "Are you?" he asked.

Dropping her eyes to his chest, she shook her head as well. He got the feeling they were both lying, but neither of them wanted to admit it.

"What do you like?" she suddenly asked.

"What?" he returned, not expecting her to ask that.

She bit down on her bottom lip and met his gaze. "Sexually. What do you like?"

His throat literally clogged up—how long had it been since he had heard that? Many, many years, certainly. There were answers, of course—lots of answers, but none that he felt comfortable enough to tell her.

His gaze darted to the phone on the night stand. Of course he had turned it off, and it hadn't magically turned itself back on and dialed her number.

Looking dejected, Willow suddenly sat down beside him on bed. "I'm sorry, I'm not good at this. I've never had to do this before and I… don't know what I'm doing. I thought that was the right thing to ask."

Instantly feeling like a heel, he sighed and said, "No, Willow, it's not that. It's not you. You're…gorgeous and wonderful and any man in the world would be lucky to be here with you right now, even just to be teased and tormented."

She stole a sideways glance at him, looking a little more uncertain. "Then what is it?"

He contemplated coming up with something or brushing it off, but he didn't want to lie to her. So, even though he knew he could be ending their little exercise early by saying so, Ethan said, "I shouldn't be here."

Not disagreeing, Willow nodded. "Probably true."

He merely nodded, not sure what else to say. All of the reasons were perfectly obvious; they didn't need to be spoken.

When he didn't continue, she added, "And yet, here you are."

"Here I am," he verified, meeting her gaze.

"If you don't… want to do this anymore, that's okay. I know it's kind of weird. I know *you* didn't need it, because you're experienced, you don't have a…bad first taste in your mouth, so to speak. But for me, this… even just the little bit that already happened… it makes me feel better. It makes me feel more confident that I will be able to regain control of my sexuality. Any discomfort I've felt since coming into this room, it hasn't been because of what happened, it's just been normal… virginal uncertainty. I don't want you to feel obligated to me in any way."

Ethan opened his mouth to respond, but he wasn't altogether sure what to say. For a moment, he said nothing, then he said, "I wish I was sitting here because I felt obligated to you in some way."

Willow looked over at him for a moment, just holding his gaze, then she stood, moved back in front of him and sat down in his lap, winding her right arm around his neck and using the other one to unbutton the top couple of buttons of his shirt.

"Touch me," she ordered.

After only the slightest hesitation, he let his hand drop to the curve of her hip, then lightly trailed his fingers down her soft leg to her kneecap. Watching her face instead of her body, he pulled his finger up the inside of her thigh, stopping just short of the hem of her panties. As he watched her, she swallowed hard, licked her lips, and looked at him again with hungry eyes that made him want to throw her down on the bed and fuck her until she was crying out his name in ecstasy.

Fuck all the reasons he couldn't do that.

Since he still wanted to, and he wasn't sure how much she wanted to be touched, he braced his hands on the edge of the bed and shoved himself backward until he wasn't so close to the edge, then he turned so that he was diagonal on the bed and lifted Willow, repositioning her so that she was straddling him.

Taking the lead, Willow finished unbuttoning his shirt and tugged it open, her brow furrowing in displeasure at the undershirt he was wearing beneath it.

Chuckling warmly, he took off the dress shirt and then pulled the undershirt over his head, tossing it bedside and taking her firmly by the hips, holding her there as he pushed against her, letting her feel his arousal. That time she didn't gasp; her fingers found the closure of his pants and she began undoing them.

Slightly alarmed, he considered telling her they should probably leave his pants on, but then, the point was that she wanted to push him however far *she* thought was far enough to prove he would still stop. So, despite his better judgment, he lifted his hips and let her slide them down his legs and off, tossing them off the side of the bed as well.

Clad only in his boxer briefs, she took a moment to just look at him. Since he made an effort to get to the gym several times a week—an effort he was happy about just then—he had maintained a lean, muscular physique. A dusting of dark hair covered his chest, but not much.

Willow ran her hands across his chest, smiling a little absently, then she leaned down, her long hair falling over her shoulder as she did, tickling his sides as she bent to place a kiss just below his collar bone. Dropping a kiss every inch or so, she made her way down his chest to his stomach, her tongue darting out when she got to his abs, leaving a hot wet trail that caused him to jerk, his erection butting up against her. When she got to the top of his waistband, she paused. Instead of continuing with her mouth, she shoved her hand down the front, taking hold of his cock and beginning a back and forth motion, firm enough that his fingers were digging into the bed sheets, but not hard enough that she was going to get him off—which he assumed was the point.

Exquisite torture.

Not grabbing her and taking control was going to kill him. Death by blue balls. Clearly he had not realized what he was signing up for.

"Does that feel good?" she asked sweetly.

"Fuck yes."

Willow grinned, seeming pleased with herself.

Then she stopped.

Apparently not satisfied with his level of discomfort, she scooted down his legs and began leaving soft kisses across his stomach again, but that time she moved her face past the hem, opened her mouth, and ran her mouth over his erection through the fabric.

Expelling something like a hiss, he moved his hands underneath his body to keep from touching her.

"Can I kiss you?" she asked quietly.

No. "Yes."

It was a line he hadn't been prepared to cross, but as she pushed her long locks back over her shoulder and pressed her warm body against his, her mouth tentatively seeking his, his brain wasn't functioning fast enough to come up with a good enough reason why not.

Her lips were soft, shy at first as she leaned more fully against him. He shifted, his hands escaping, gravitating to her body, one lightly caressing its way up her back, the other moving to cup her face, then trail around the back of her head to tug her closer. The kiss she was giving him was nice, but if he was going to cross the line, he wanted a little more than that.

Her body tensed slightly when she felt his tongue, but she opened her mouth just a little and kissed him back. Desire coiled in his loins as she deepened the kiss he had initiated, lust making him ache as Willow rested a hand on his shoulder and the other found his hair again, her fingers making their way through the soft, dark mass. Her kiss turned a little more frantic, her tongue a little bolder. When she started moaning, grinding against his cock, he thought he might explode in the more literal sense.

Before he realized what he meant to do, his hands found the clasp of her bra and he unfastened it; she didn't object, didn't even break the kiss as she let go of him to finish taking the damn thing off.

And then her breasts were free, and as his palm connected with the first one, she pushed it against him even harder—eager. She was breathing hard, squirming, moaning, and the thought flitted through his mind that if he asked her right then, she would probably let him fuck her.

But she wasn't thinking.

So he didn't ask.

When she finally broke the kiss to come up for air, he could see the frustration on her face—she was turned on, just as much as he was.

Obviously she hadn't accounted for that.

Before she had a chance to resume the kiss, he put both hands behind her bare back and pressed her up against him until he had the peak of one breast between his lips. Her body arched as he trapped it between his teeth and she released a helpless little moan, tilting her head back and closing her eyes as his mouth closed around her nipple and his tongue began to play with it.

Then she brought her own hand up to cup the other one—squeezing, kneading herself, and one of the hands on her back lost control, his nails lightly scoring her skin as he dragged them down her back. She gasped in surprise, but then little noises of pleasure escaped her and there was no sign of displeasure—none whatsoever.

When he released her breast, she opened her eyes and looked at him, her eyes a little wild, and then she was on him again, pressing her pelvis against his cock purposefully, her mouth devouring his. After she ground against him a few more times, *he* actually had to stop *her*, because he was dangerously close to coming.

"Do you want to stop?" he asked.

He barely let out the question and she ground out, "No."

"Can I touch you?"

"You can do anything you want to me," she said a touch breathlessly.

Jesus Christ, as if he wasn't turned on enough already.

Since she had said that though, he figured he could take just a little more leeway. Flipping her over so that her back was against the bed and he was above her, he replied, "How's that?"

"Mm hmm," she murmured, nodding her head.

Ethan bent to take a breast in his mouth, figuring he should keep her warmed up and frustrated for a minute, and she was just as responsive as she had been before—which was damn sexy.

After a minute, he pulled back, crawling back a little and hooking his fingers inside of the hem of her panties. He looked up at her, raising an eyebrow questioningly, and she lifted her hips, her right hand coming down to shove the panties off herself, since he wasn't doing it fast enough.

Still writhing beneath him, even when he was barely touching her, Willow was the very picture of sexual eagerness. His cock throbbed, begging him to take advantage of her current state of pliancy—she said *anything*, after all, and she was horny enough that he would bet his house that she wouldn't turn down his cock.

If only he didn't have a fucking conscience.

Instead of pursuing their mutual pleasure, he decided to hold up his end of the bargain—even if she didn't want him to.

"Fuck," he muttered.

Willow glanced up at him, but she didn't seem to register what he said.

He might as well make it good for one of them.

Flashing her a devilish smile, he moved down the bed, gripping her thighs and spreading them. Ducking his head between her legs, he used his thumbs to spread her lips, and then his mouth was covering her, his tongue moving inside of her as she moaned, and that time *her* fingers were digging into the sheets.

Once he found the spot that had her whimpering, he didn't let go, holding onto her to keep her from squirming so much as his tongue lapped at her and her cries became more desperate. Her body twisted and the sounds she was making were driving him crazy; then he felt her lose herself, her body convulsing as she cried out in pleasure.

Spent, she fell limply against the bed. Ethan climbed up beside her, lying on his back and trying to concentrate on getting his own arousal under control.

Willow turned on her side and curled up against him, the hand she had resting on his chest moving down his stomach, stopping at his still-painful erection.

He winced a little, and she pushed her hand down the front, curled her fingers around the base, and began stroking him.

"Do you want me to go down on you?" she asked.

Every fiber of his being was screaming yes, but he forced himself to shake his head no. "It's okay," he said, attempting a smile. "This was the plan all along."

"I know, but… it seems so mean now."

His smile widened, becoming a little more genuine despite his discomfort. "It's okay, I deserve it."

She brushed her lips against his chest, then she sat up and moved down his body anyway, tugging the underwear down his hips.

"No, Willow." If the boxers came off, he wasn't going to be able to resist. "Really. Come here."

His voice was strained even to his own ears, but she glanced uncertainly at his erection, then obediently came back up to lie beside him, seeming perfectly content when he wrapped an arm around her.

She was quiet for about half a minute, then she said, "I told you that you could do anything you wanted to me."

"Mm hmm. And I did."

"You only wanted to go down on me?"

"No, I only wanted to give you pleasure. I think I did...?" he trailed off, flashing her a teasing smile.

Fanning herself in an exaggerated manner, she grinned. "I'll say."

She curled up even closer, tangling one of her legs between his. They were quiet for a couple minutes, then Willow said, "Ethan?"

"Yeah?"

"Why didn't you want to fuck me?"

He was *just* getting his cock under control and she had to go and say something like that. "I very much wanted to fuck you, Willow."

"Then why didn't you?"

She wasn't looking up at him—probably not wanting to make eye contact while she asked questions like that, but he needed her to look at him when he answered, so he hooked a finger beneath her chin and tugged it upward. She tilted her head back, her gray eyes meeting his gaze.

"You deserve for your first time to be with someone you care about."

She attempted a half-ass smile, but it didn't reach her eyes. "You were already my first, Ethan."

"No," he disagreed, shaking his head. "I wasn't. Forget the…technical stuff. The first person you *give yourself* to… it shouldn't be me, and it shouldn't be like this."

Instead of sensibly agreeing with him, she showed her age by asking, "Why not you?"

Offering his own sad, half-ass smile, he said, "'Cause I'm not available. I can't give you what you deserve. You'll have to find someone else to do that."

She looked a bit glum, but she nodded, so at least she understood the truth of his words, even if—in the moment, sated and naked in his arms—she was not very happy about it.

It would pass.

And then she would be glad she hadn't made that mistake.

And his cock would just have to fucking deal with it.

# CHAPTER FIFTEEN

Willow was having a fantastic dream.

It was a weird version of her dream—it had started out at her house the night she had been abducted, but instead of the bad guys, Ethan was at the door, and instead of drugging or stealing her away in the night to some house of horrors, he kissed her and stole her away to a place of pleasure.

Her eyes eased open and the room was dark. Momentarily disoriented, she tried to figure out why her bedroom window wasn't where she remembered it being, and why her pillow was so…warm and…body-like.

Then her eyes popped open in the dark and she reached out to verify that yes, she was lying beside a human man.

And it was Ethan.

Holy shit.

Okay, that made sense. The sleep-fog was clearing, and she remembered that she had been lying in bed with Ethan at the hotel—she must have fallen asleep. He must have too, although since the room was dark and there had been lights on before she fell asleep, she assumed he must have gotten up at some point. How odd that he would let her sleep, and even more peculiar that he would stick around when he should probably be getting home.

What time was it?

Her purse was all the way in the bathroom, and she had no desire to move from the warm comfort of Ethan's embrace to go get it and find out.

God, it was like being in heaven. It wasn't like it was the first time she had cuddled, but it was definitely *different* with him.

Better.

Shaking that thought off, she closed her eyes and contented herself to just lie there with his arms around her— very likely the last time that would ever happen, and almost as likely, the last time she would ever be alone with him.

Despite his insistence that he didn't feel obligated and he *had* wanted to fuck her, she was reasonably sure that if a guy who was already turned on and lusting after her turned her down when she offered sex…he was lying.

She wasn't *that* naïve.

The guys she *had* gotten close with would not have hesitated long enough to let her finish her sentence if she would have granted them permission.

Not that she blamed him. Although she didn't like to think of it anymore, Ethan had a whole life that she wasn't a part of, and of course he wouldn't want to risk that.

Not that she wanted him to or anything....

Still, it stung just a little.

Actually, more than a little.

As if he could sense her thoughts, Ethan shifted in his sleep, letting go of her and rolling over, turning his back to her.

Inexplicably, that made her sad.

The contentment was gone, and in its place she felt restless and uncomfortable. Maybe the night had worn out its welcome.

Of course, Ethan was her ride home, so it wasn't like she could just leave.

After lying there for a few more minutes with the same thoughts running through her head, she rolled out of the bed and padded across the room, accidentally kicking her purse, which had been placed in front of the mini-fridge along with her clothes, neatly folded and placed on the ground. She picked it all up, clutching it to her chest, and went into the bathroom, closing the door and turning on the way-too-bright light.

Digging her cell phone out, she was thankful to still have some battery left, so she was able to send a text message. Setting the phone down, she focused on getting all of her clothes back on. Thankfully, her phone buzzed a moment later.

Quickly tapping out a reply, she pushed send and then turned the light off, walking out into the room, which was suddenly even darker than it had been before her eyes adjusted to the bathroom.

She wasn't sure she had everything.

Her clothes were all on, she had her phone and her purse… it seemed like she had brought more with her, but she knew she didn't.

She was just reluctant to leave the room.

Reluctant to leave him.

Dammit.

Since she still had a little time, she made her way over to the chair beside the bed and took a seat, placing her purse on the ottoman and resting her elbow on her leg, leaning on her palm as she gazed at Ethan, lying in bed asleep.

She should probably wake him up. Of course, by 4:15 am, his wife had probably figured out he wasn't coming home—and she was sure he had a suitable excuse, since the truth obviously wouldn't work in that scenario—but he might need to set an alarm or something.

But then he would have to come up with something suitable to say to *her*, and she didn't want lies. The truth would be worse.

No words. She didn't need words.

True to his word, even despite her own desires, he *had* proven what she asked him to prove to her. Even when she *didn't* say no, he was able to stop.

That was good.

For some reason, it didn't *feel* good, but logically she knew it was. Her brain just wasn't working right—probably from lack of sleep.

Yeah, that was it.

Her phone lit up eventually and she stood, sighing as she took one last look at him. She wished she could encapsulate the moment, even though she knew logically it meant nothing.

Illogically, it felt like it did.

To her, anyway.

She knew that was stupid. She *knew* that.

So, with one last look, she made her way out of the hotel room, down the corridor, and out the door. The maroon sedan was parked right in front of it, the lights still on, waiting for her.

As she opened up the door and slid inside, hugging herself against the chilly early morning air, Willow glanced over with a sheepish smile. "Thanks."

Her brother nodded his head, flicking a glance at the hotel door, but he didn't ask any questions.

She loved him for that.

The only thing he asked, as he put the car in reverse, was, "You okay?"

Injecting false brightness into voice, she said, "Yeah, I'm fine."

Todd nodded, accepting her answer, and made his way toward the exit.

Before they pulled out, Willow glanced back, just to make sure Ethan hadn't come rushing out to see where she went.

Of course he didn't, so she turned to face the front.

"You sure?" her brother asked.

"I'm great," she assured him, nodding her head.

Looking even less convinced than before, he offered another nod but didn't ask again.

# CHAPTER SIXTEEN

Ethan hadn't heard from Willow since the night they had spent together—at least, he knew they spent *part* of it together.

It was nearly 5 am when he woke up, and Willow had already fled.

He may not have thought of it as fleeing, except she hadn't spoken to him since.

Not really.

The next day, as soon as he thought she might be awake and he had a spare moment, he sent her a text to just see how she was doing.

Her response had been, "fine."

That was it.

The last thing she had ever said to him.

He had no goddamn idea why. When he had fallen asleep, everything had been okay. She certainly hadn't seemed *mad* at him.

That was the only reason he could come up with for not hearing from her though.

He still kept tabs on her, even though he knew he shouldn't. Especially because every time he checked on her, there were new pictures of her with a different dipshit on her arm.

Every time he looked, it soured his mood, yet he found himself checking every goddamn weekend.

Logically, he knew he should consider himself lucky. He managed to get away with things he *knew* people weren't supposed to get away with. Instead of losing everything, he had somehow managed to keep his family together, not get thrown in jail, and then Willow turned out to be fucking perfect, not only forgiving him, but striking up a friendship and then offering him *her body*, of all things. Then, quiet as could be, she disappeared afterward.

Nobody was that lucky.

Nobody.

He knew the other shoe had to be out there somewhere, just waiting to smack him in the head as it fell.

Jarring him out of his thoughts, Amanda's fingers grazed his arm, then she curled her arm around him. He was lying in bed with his back facing her, but she tugged on his arm, so he rolled over onto his back and peered at her curiously.

She smiled at him. "Hey you. I thought you might be asleep."

"Nah." It was a ridiculous notion. Now that he wasn't losing sleep over his first transgression, he had new ones to keep him up at night.

Sleep.

Sleep was for the innocent.

Apparently pleased at his sleeplessness, Amanda pulled herself up closer to him and leaned in for a kiss. He obliged, even though he couldn't remember the last time she had given him a good night kiss, but then he realized she wasn't looking for a good night kiss—she was interested in a bit more than that.

Not sure exactly what to do, he lazily rested an arm around her waist and kissed her back, but he couldn't seem to stay in one place—his lips were on Amanda's, but his mind was flying back to that hotel room with Willow.

It was like there was a vat of guilt, liquefied, roiling around in the pit of his stomach.

After a minute, Amanda pulled back. He felt a little relieved, releasing her and letting his hand drop back to his side of the bed. He offered her a tiny, pointless smile, and she frowned as she sat back in her own spot.

"What's wrong with you?" Amanda asked, crossing her arms over her chest.

"What do you mean?"

"You're never in the mood anymore." Averting her gaze, she said, "I've finally lost most of my baby weight and you haven't even noticed. I thought you'd be...interested again."

"I was never not interested, honey. Not because of— how could you think that?"

"What else could I think?" she demanded, her voice dipping a little. "You certainly haven't… I feel like you aren't attracted to me anymore."

"Of course I am," he said, pulling her into his arms.

"Doesn't seem like it," she muttered sadly. "Why won't you tell me what's going on with you, Ethan?"

He knew that it was *the* opening to tell her any version of the truth, to get it out in the open and try to explain it to her. As terrible a thought as it was, he even figured if she was feeling a little insecure, she might be more inclined to forgive him...if he only told part of the truth.

He was sure she wouldn't forgive him if she knew all of it.

Pretty sure, anyway.

It seemed pointless to only tell half the truth though. It would only hurt her, and especially if he had made her feel like that, he didn't want to make it worse by telling her he had nearly slept with another woman.

He was just being a shitty everything lately. Obviously a shitty husband, but he had hoped she wouldn't notice. Of course she noticed.

"Listen to me," he said, in lieu of the truth. "I'm sorry that I made you feel that way. But you need to know, *no part* of how I've been lately has anything to do with you."

"Then what is it?" she asked, frowning up at him. "Talk to me, Ethan."

Since he couldn't—wouldn't—he shut down instead. "I don't want an argument, Amanda. I'm tired."

Baffled, she said, "I wasn't *arguing*, I just—"

"We can talk about it tomorrow, okay?" he said, rolling over.

Of course they wouldn't.

Heaving a sigh of irritation, she made a point to violently yank her blanket up and squirm around before finally getting comfortable.

Ethan closed his eyes and dreaded the day she would push him until he cracked.

It had to be coming.

It just had to be.

---

"Pick up milk."

Ethan sighed and dropped his phone in the cup holder, turning his signal on and turning around as soon as he was able.

It had been a boring-ass day at work, nobody wanted to misbehave when it was convenient for him to catch them, and he had accomplished pretty much nothing.

Consequently, he left early.

It slipped his mind to tell Amanda—which never used to happen, so that was his fault.

After he parked the car, he texted her to ask if they needed anything else while he was there, then he got out, slipping his keys into his pocket and headed inside the grocery store.

A moment later, she told him to see if they had a pumpkin carving kit since he never found the one he swore he put in the top of the closet last year.

Since he had no damn idea where that thing was, he made note of it.

Once he was in the Halloween aisle, he figured he would get an extra bag of candy just in case they ran out. Alison snuck the miniature peanut butter cups every time she thought someone wasn't looking.

Candy under arm and new carving set in hand, he turned around and headed for the milk.

"I think we need Twizzlers."

His head jerked up at the sound of Willow's voice. There she was, walking down the aisle in his direction wearing a pair of snug jeans, a black top, and a burgundy jacket. She wasn't looking in his direction though, she was looking over at the teenager walking beside her—a scrawny blonde kid who was staring down at his cell phone while he walked.

"She's not coming," Scrawny said.

Willow rolled her eyes. "Lame. Tell her she's lame. We still need Twizzlers."

Then she looked up and came to an abrupt stop when she spotted Ethan standing at the end of the aisle, looking at her.

"Uh, hi," she said, a touch awkwardly.

The kid beside her glanced up, but apparently lost interest on sight, looking back down at his cell phone.

"Hi," he returned, none too smoothly himself. "How are you?"

She smiled a little, but it wasn't a look of amusement—maybe *at* him, but certainly not *with* him. "Fine. I'm fine."

"Right," he said, remembering the text. He couldn't expand on that with the kid standing there.

As if reading his mind, Willow lightly rested her hand on the arm of the kid next to her. His head jerked up in surprise and Willow spoke before he could.

"Hey, you know what, I bet we're going to need a basket. Could you go get one?"

Nodding, he took one last glance in Ethan's direction and then turned to go do Willow's bidding.

Ethan smiled a little, but his didn't feel real either. "Neat trick. Do you give him a treat when he comes back?"

"Only if he doesn't slobber," she deadpanned.

Ethan scoffed a bit, but maintained his smile. "Makes sense. Do you have any female friends, or…?"

Her smile turned a little more knowing then. "Why do you assume we're only friends?"

"Are you seriously trying to make me jealous with a fucking kid?" Shaking his head, irritated with himself immediately, he said, "Nope, never mind, I didn't—never mind."

Willow laughed. "God, Ethan, we're not awkward exes. And I'm not trying to make you jealous—like I knew you would be at the grocery store. You're right, I did! I just sit outside your house every night waiting for you to leave, and if you do, I go round up the nearest guy and see if I can run into you. I can't believe this is the first time it's worked."

"Why were you pissed at me?" he asked, before he could think better of it.

Her smile waned. "I wasn't pissed."

"You seem a little pissed."

Lifting her eyebrows, she said, "Um, no. You're the one being aggressive with me because I came to the grocery store with a boy. You have a wife. You *cannot* be serious. And you didn't want to fuck me anyway, so I'm not sure why it matters."

Darting a glance in each direction to make sure no one overheard her, he looked at her pointedly and said, "Want to keep it down?"

She shrugged, but lowered her voice and stepped a little closer. "I don't know what your problem is. You did your penance or whatever, you don't have to feel guilty anymore, okay? I release you," she said, wiggling her fingers in the air as if doing magic.

"I told you—" He sighed heavily, shaking his head. Women could be so exhausting.

"It's fine," she assured him, offering a less sarcastic smile that time. "We're cool."

"You don't seem cool."

"*You* don't seem cool."

Since he had absolutely no argument, he nodded his head. "You're right. I'm sorry. I didn't mean to—I was just surprised, I didn't expect to see you."

She nodded, seeming to accept his apology, her gaze drifting to the pumpkin carving kit. "Getting ready for Halloween?"

"Yep," he replied, but inexplicably, he still felt a little sullen himself. Not that it was her fault, but seeing her with that kid reminded him of his own problems at home, which reminded him of not only the hotel, but the *very* start of all his fucking problems, and Willow was at the center of all of it.

Not to blame, but still the center of the storm.

Ethan sighed.

Willow frowned and stepped a little closer, putting a hand on his arm. "Hey, are you okay?"

Producing a little smile, he said, "Your tricks won't work on me."

She laughed shortly. "Keep telling yourself that."

There was no malice though—she actually winked at him.

Well, fuck. Seeing her just made him aware that he actually *missed* her.

He didn't mean to say anything else—apparently he was doing and saying all kinds of things he didn't mean that day—but he asked, "Why didn't you ever text me again?"

She opened her mouth to respond, but then her gaze jerked up behind him and she released his arm, not moving immediately, but taking on a more demure smile and then shifting away much more subtly. "Well, tell her I said hi."

• • •
*218*

That was an odd response—the kid had obviously dismissed him, he wasn't going to be suspicious that she had stopped to talk to him. Hell, he could be anybody.

Then the kid returned to Willow's side without a basket, and her mother—the fun one, at least—rounded the corner and said enthusiastically, "Well, hello there!"

Fuck.

Pasting on a polite smile, Ethan turned and saw Lauren wheeling a cart in his direction, a few containers of fruit punch rolling around in the front.

"Hi," he said casually, nodding his head. "How are you?"

"Great," she said cheerily. "We're just picking up a few things for Willow's party—she's having a Halloween party."

"Oh, that sounds like fun."

Smiling brightly, she bobbed her head. "We think so. I would invite you, but it's kids only."

"Mom," Willow drawled, shooting her mother a look of annoyance.

"Sorry, sorry, not kids—he knew what I meant."

The correct assumption, since he was an adult. He glanced at Willow, and she shook her head very slightly, clearly perturbed.

Well, sure. It was awkward when you knew what they knew. No way her mother would see them as peers.

"So, it was nice seeing you," Ethan said, preparing to make his escape. "I'm glad everything's…" He trailed off, but they both merely nodded. With a blanket wave, he turned and headed toward the milk.

Before he got out of earshot, he heard the scrawny kid mutter, "He doesn't look like a PI."

Willow's mom merely laughed, while Willow fell silent.

He wondered if she was brooding. It was disturbing how quickly she turned into a teenager when her mother was in the picture—not her fault, of course; she *was* a teenager, but he just didn't think of her that way when she wasn't directly beside a parent figure.

Feeling a little uncomfortable, he grabbed the milk and made a beeline for the register before he ran into them again.

# CHAPTER SEVENTEEN

The harder she tried not to think of Ethan, the more she did.

Justin, her friend from the day before, had refused to dress up for the costume party since he didn't think he would look cool enough. After the grocery store, he had the bright-ass idea to show up with a name tag that said, "Ethan Wilde" and claim he was dressed up as a PI.

Fucking hilarious.

The party itself had been her mom's idea. Since Willow seemed to be "normalizing" a bit more, her mom thought a party was a good idea.

It wasn't. Willow knew that, but she figured she would humor her mother—it was only one night, after all. Hopefully it would be a good one.

As she suspected, that was not to be.

Yes, she was fine with socializing again, but then a couple of the guys wanted to bring some girl she didn't know, and then someone else was inviting this other guy she didn't know, and as soon as there were strangers in her house, Willow was instantly uncomfortable.

She did not trust strangers. Not even teenage ones.

It didn't take long before some guy dressed in a wife-beater, saggy pants, and a backward baseball cap sat on the couch beside her—clearly he was dressed as a douchebag for Halloween—and said, "So, are you like the only single girl here?"

Giving him her most withering glare, she felt some satisfaction when he held up his hands in surrender, got up, and left her alone.

Since her party had been overtaken, Willow snuck up to her room as soon as she could and shut herself inside, pulling her witch's hat off and tossing it on the bed before flopping down beside it.

Yawning, she wished she could just curl up in bed and take a nap, but she knew her prolonged absence would be noticed.

She pulled out her phone, checking the time, and wondered if it would be okay to text Ethan. Usually it seemed to be, but she didn't understand why he never seemed worried about getting text messages at home, especially in the evening.

Then again, maybe getting calls after nine wasn't so odd in his line of work.

"Guess who Justin dressed up as?" she finally sent.

A moment later, he answered, "I don't know who Justin is."

"The fucking kid."

"Oh, him. A bodybuilder."

Cracking a smile, she said, "Ethan Wilde, PI!"

"Oh, but I don't like look a PI," he answered.

"That's true, you don't even wear a trench coat."

A minute passed with no response, then it showed him typing. "What are you wearing?"

Her eyebrows shot up in surprise.

"For a costume!" he added quickly.

She made a little winking face and sent back, "Nothing."

"That's mean."

"JK. I'm a witch."

Then, since she had a camera at her disposal, she hopped off the bed and went into the bathroom to take a mirror selfie in her admittedly sexy purple and black witch costume. It did amazing things for her cleavage.

After he saw it, he replied, "How many guys have asked you if you want a ride on their broomstick?"

Laughing out loud, she said, "You're the first, congratulations!" Then she added, "Some strange guy was about to hit on me, but apparently only because I'm the only single girl here."

"Excellent strategy," he replied.

"I didn't do it on purpose."

"Sure you didn't."

There was a knock at her door and she made her way out of the bathroom just as Ashlynn opened up the door.

"There you are," she said. "What are you doing up here?"

The phone was still in her hand, which made her feel weirdly guilty, but Willow merely shrugged. "I had to go to the bathroom. Someone was in the other one."

Grabbing her hat off the bed, she placed it back on her head and followed Ashlynn out of her room, pulling the door closed behind her.

---

"I think we should have a date night."

Ethan was in his office, very much not expecting Amanda to appear in the doorway.

"Okay," he said slowly. "We can do that."

"Tonight. Let's go to dinner—we can go into the city."

"We don't have a sitter," he said, brow furrowing.

"I called Brandi, she's free." Offering up a smile, she said, "Come on, it'll be fun and impulsive. We haven't been out alone since before Caleb was born."

"You know I don't like Brandi."

Amanda rolled her eyes. "Brandi's fine, you just don't want to go out. Come on, I'm going to go get dressed while you finish up in here."

Even though he didn't like the babysitter, he agreed. It was probably a good idea, and he was actually a little surprised he hadn't thought of it himself. Although… she might try to get him to *talk* at dinner. It could be a trick.

Oh well, he could evade that, no problem.

Closing his email, he opened up his desk drawer and pulled out a file, then spun around and grabbed a few papers off the printer tray, stacking them neatly and pushing them inside the folder.

His cell phone was lying on the desk and it lit up just before he looked at it.

It was Willow. "I want Chinese food!!"

Smiling slightly, he grabbed the phone and sent back, "Go get some."

"Maybe I should. Are you doing anything?"

Faltering a little, he stared at the phone for a few seconds, then he impulsively closed the message and put the phone back on the desk.

A few minutes later, after he had everything filed away, he touched his phone and saw a message, a couple minutes old. "Busy?"

He sent back simply, "Yeah, sorry."

"No problem. Working?"

Again, he stared at the damn phone. He should just say yes, that would be easiest. The truth couldn't be a good idea, right?

Or maybe it was.

Maybe it was *exactly* the right answer.

His Willow problem had evolved; initially it had been so much worse because he had hurt her, but it seemed like more of an affair at that point... and that was a much simpler fix.

*Maybe* he could get away with coming halfway clean, after all. Willow had let him off the hook time and again, and he really didn't think about it a lot anymore since she had proven such an overall distraction... so maybe that was the ticket.

If he was just honest with Amanda about that, she would be pissed at him, yes, but maybe then he wouldn't feel so shitty and secretive all the time.

Maybe it was time to cut Willow loose. He had never intended for that to turn into a relationship to begin with, he'd only wanted to help her.

Part of him hated that idea—he would miss Willow if he never heard from her again. He would also hate to hurt her feelings again, since it seemed like he had before.

Before he could talk himself out of it, he quickly typed, "Date night."

The phone showed that she read the message, but no matter how many minutes he sat there staring at it, no message was typed back.

He eventually regretted sending it. If he would have regretted it fast enough, maybe he could have turned it into a joke or something, but… he had not.

Muttering a curse at himself, he finally gave up waiting for a response—he wasn't sure why he expected one—and shoved his cell phone in his pocket, going out to spend a little time with the kids before the sitter got there.

---

Ethan was not surprised when, the day after his date text, he checked Willow's page and saw a picture of her with a new addition to her parade of horny teenage guys. He told himself that was a good sign, she was moving on, he was moving on—although he had not come clean to Amanda, despite the golden opportunity to do so—and the situation was finally resolving itself.

That seemed to be the case, too. She didn't text him again after he sent that one, and all night he had checked his phone to make sure.

Things at home did not magically return to normal. There was no discernible difference, with one exception: his dreams about Willow came back.

Not the good ones. Not the real memories of the night at the hotel, or the imaginary ones about fucking her in the Jacuzzi, but the vivid, tear-filled, unpleasant ones from that one night in that goddamn house with those assholes crowded around, watching him hurt her.

When he woke up, he was surly as hell. He couldn't even remember the last time he had one like that, and when he woke up with a fucking hard-on, it soured his mood for the whole day.

That bullshit was supposed to be over.

He didn't even check her accounts that day. He felt too shitty to look at her face, even through a computer screen.

Finally, right before bed, he decided to try to bait his mind—if he was going to have sex dreams about Willow, he would at least like to remember something consensual, so he went to look for the picture of her in the witch costume.

Then he noticed something he hadn't been paying attention to before—game posts. In the middle of the night. That previous night, from around 1:30 to 4:15 she had been awake playing some game, posting requests that were all in a little game box that he hadn't noticed before because he was so busy watching for pictures like an asshole.

What a fucking idiot.

Scrolling back, he saw the posts had been like that several nights—not all in a row, she skipped a day or two now and then, and it would only go back to the most recent 100 requests, so if she had been doing it for longer, there was no record.

Willow wasn't sleeping.

Sinking back into his chair, he felt like all of the progress he thought they made had been wiped away.

Had she been having the dreams all along? And if she was, frankly, how the hell was she able to talk to him?

Sitting forward, he went back to the recent pictures she had posted, but none were up close enough so that he could see if she had circles under her eyes.

Maybe he hadn't helped her with a damn thing, and he was just kidding himself. Maybe she was just letting him think that because she was the nicest person in the entire world.

Picking up his phone, he scrolled through his messages before remembering that he had deleted the whole thread. Every trace of her.

What a dickhead he was. There he was, worrying about an affair, and she was probably still suffering from brutal memories in the middle of the night.

Opening up a new message, he typed in her phone number and then hovered, trying to figure out what to say. If he asked if she was okay, she would just assure him that she was fine.

After debating for a few minutes, he finally came up with, "I could sure use some Chinese right now…"

The message didn't immediately register as read, so he put it down and waited. A few minutes passed without response, so he opened his computer and decided to check his email one more time, which led to three other things he hadn't planned on doing.

Suddenly a half hour had passed and still no response. That was unusual for her, so he checked the message again…and saw that she had read the message twenty minutes earlier.

No response.

That surprised him for a minute, but then when he thought about it with his new theories about her sleeping habits, he realized maybe it shouldn't.

Why had he stopped checking on her when things had turned sexual? What a stupid thing to do.

Well, no, actually, she had been the one to dip out, hadn't she? The morning after the hotel, he *had* contacted her, but she ignored him. Then he didn't see or talk to her again until the grocery store, then Halloween, which he assumed was because she saw him *at* the grocery store.

He was so confused.

Figuring he would wait a little while longer just in case she changed her mind, he lost close to an hour doing absolutely nothing on the internet, and would have wasted more time if not for Amanda coming to the door with the cordless phone and telling him he had a call.

Everything froze for a split second. Willow wouldn't actually call his house, would she? How would she have even gotten the phone number? But *nobody* called the house for him, and Amanda sounded vaguely irritated.

Preparing to open the door to an understandably furious woman, he was surprised when Amanda merely handed him the phone and turned to walk back down the hall.

His shoulders went slack in relief and he put the phone to his ear. "Hello."

"I've been trying to reach you—did you change your fucking number?"

Frowning, Ethan asked, "Who is this?"

"It's fucking Tito, man, who you think?"

That was so much worse than what he had prepared for.

"What the hell are you doing calling my house phone?" Ethan demanded in a furious whisper. "How did you get this fucking number?"

"I need to talk to you, man. I'm in a real bad scrape."

Amanda had stopped at the end of the hall and turned around, walking back in his direction. Although she didn't typically attempt to eavesdrop, that was the time she just stood there watching him.

"I can't talk right now. Don't call me at this number again, I will call you back on a different line."

When he hangs up, Amanda frowns. "Who was that?"

"Nobody," he muttered.

"*Nobody*? Do you usually swear at nobody? Who shouldn't be calling you at home?"

"*Nobody* should be calling me at home, that's why I have three fucking cell phones," he stated irritably.

"What's going on?" she asked, her brow furrowing even more in concern. "Who was that man, Ethan?"

"I…" He shook his head, then realized he hadn't taken Tito's number. The chances of him having the same phone probably weren't very good. Cursing again, he tried to see if he called from a listed number, but of course he hadn't.

Ethan shook his head. "I need to get a new job."

She laughed a little. "No kidding."

Apparently satisfied that it was a client, Amanda turned and headed back down the hall while Ethan went back to his office, Willow's problems all but forgotten.

# CHAPTER EIGHTEEN

Caleb was sleeping peacefully on his chest, and as much as Ethan wanted to leave him there, he also needed to pee *really* badly.

Eventually, his bladder won out and he got to his feet, shushing and swaying as he walked to put the baby back to sleep when he started to flail.

By the time he got to the bedroom, Caleb was asleep again, so he put him down in the crib, turned on the monitor, and made for the bathroom.

As he was washing his hands, he felt his pocket buzzing. Quickly drying them off, he pulled his phone out and saw that Willow was *calling* him.

That was unusual—and she had never answered his text about the Chinese food, so he thought she didn't want to talk to him—so he frowned as he slid his finger across the screen and put the phone to his ear.

"Hello?" he answered, not bothering to mask his surprise.

"Hey," she returned, as casually as if she called him every day.

Hoping to find out why she called without asking, he asked, "Everything okay?"

"Yeah, everything's...fine."

"Good," he said inanely, then waited.

Sighing audibly, she said, "So, I'm just going to throw this out there... I'm home by myself, I will be for several hours, but a girl's gotta eat, so I'm making dinner. I made *way* too much, and... I don't know, I thought I'd see if maybe you want to come over?"

"To your house?" he reiterated.

"Yes. My brother's not home and my parents are in Chicago, nobody will know you were here."

The correct response was no. He didn't know why when he opened his mouth, what spilled out was a teasing, "I don't think all your boyfriends would like that."

She laughed, and he smiled at the sound. "*All* of my boyfriends? Have you been stalking me, Ethan?"

"You should expect as much given my line of work," he returned lightly.

"That's adorable," she stated. "Unfounded, but absolutely adorable. Are you coming over or what?"

"I...I really shouldn't."

"Okay," she said brightly. "Well, I just thought I'd ask."

He hadn't expected that—didn't know why he hadn't expected that—but her easy acceptance made him realize he *wanted* to go. Chuckling, he said, "Well, if you're gonna twist my arm like that…"

"It's no big deal," she informed him, sweet as honey. "I can just invite my army of boyfriends over to help me eat it all."

A snort escaped before he could catch it. "Your army of boyfriends, huh?"

"Well, the ones on active duty, of course. Not the reserves."

"You have reserves, too?" he asked, playing along.

"Of course. I'm a girl—we all have reserves."

"Well, don't I feel special. Am I one of your reserves?"

"Why do you assume I count you among the ranks at all?" she teased.

"Oh, I see how you are. That's cold," he replied, despite his grin.

"Hey, if you wanna stay in the reserves, you have to at least talk to me once in a while, put in a little effort."

He knew that game—she was pretending to be joking, saying it all light and playful, but she was not joking. Not all the way, at least.

"Hey, I just asked you out for Chinese not that long ago, I never heard back."

"Aw, yeah. Sorry. That was a date night."

Ethan rolled his eyes, even though it probably wasn't even a lie—she probably had gone out with someone.

"What time?"

"What time…what?"

"When should I be there?" he specified.

"Ooh, you changed your mind? Okay, I guess you can still come."

"You didn't make other plans in the last ten seconds?"

"I know, I'm such a loser," she joked. "You can come whenever. Dinner will be done in a little over an hour and the house is clear already, so…"

He told her he would leave in a few minutes, then as he headed into the other room to tell Amanda he was going out, he tried not to feel like a huge asshole.

Given that her dinner invitation had appeared out of the blue, he wasn't sure what to expect. He wasn't exactly sure where they stood, and judging from the way she danced around in front of the door after letting him in, she wasn't either.

"I brought wine," he said, holding up a small paper bag.

"Good call," she said with a nod.

"Just in case. I wasn't sure…."

"No, that'll be good. I made eggplant parmesan and got stuff ready for salads, but I wasn't sure how you liked yours. We have French, Italian, and ranch dressing, so if you don't like one of those, you are out of luck."

Letting his gaze wander over her, he felt a little underdressed in his jeans and black sweater. Along with a pair of black heels, Willow was wearing the snug black dress with a shoulder-baring, red gauzy top—the one she had posted a while back, before things had become even more complicated between them. It looked even better in person.

Then she turned and gestured for him to follow her into the living room, and he saw that the dress zipped all the way up the back.

His fingers itched to unzip it.

Taking a seat on the couch, she patted the cushion beside her and he followed her cue and sat down, placing the bag with the wine in the floor next to the couch.

"You look very pretty," he told her, absently reaching out to run a finger along her bare shoulder.

"Thank you," she said, giving him a little smile. "So do you."

"Ugh, I couldn't find a thing to wear," he joked. "Everything made me look fat."

Rolling her eyes in amusement, she said, "Yeah, I bet you have that problem all the time."

"Constantly," he murmured, his focus waning as she leaned back against the couch, her hair fanning out behind her, and tilted her head to look up at him with something close to admiration. Smiling slightly, he asked, "What's that look for?"

"What look?" she asked innocently, her not-so-innocent right hand brushing across his leg to land on the inside of his thigh.

"I thought you were supposed to be mad at me."

Instead of confirming or denying that, her hand moved inward even more until she was rubbing him through the fabric of his jeans.

Ethan leaned his head back and closed his eyes as his pants became uncomfortably tight. Willow shifted, turning so that she had a better angle, and then climbed on top of him, hiking her dress up so she could straddle him.

His hands found her thighs, pushing up under the dress and cupping his hand between her legs. Smiling a little, she reached for the button of his jeans.

"I thought I was here for dinner," he managed.

"You are. Why not have a little dessert first?" She flashed him her minx-like smile and then she was kissing him, and God help him, he locked his arm around her waist, pulling her close, and kissed her back.

With his hand between her legs he went for her panties—only to find she wasn't wearing any. Groaning against her mouth, he slid a finger inside of her and she moaned, catching his bottom lip between her teeth and lightly biting him.

Pulling back from the kiss, he leaned in to brush his lips along the curve of her neck as she tilted it to give him better access. "Did you invite me here to fuck you?"

"Maybe," she whispered, shoving her fingers through his hair. "Would you complain if I did?"

In lieu of an answer, he pushed a second finger inside of her, causing her to squirm in his lap.

Since his hand was already around her back and that dress was just begging to be stripped off of her, he went for the zipper, watching her face as he tugged it halfway down her back.

"Take the top part off," he commanded.

She smiled at that, and proceeded to do just what he asked, tugging the sleeves off so that her black lacy bra was the only thing hiding her breasts.

"Now the bra."

Squirming a little as he continued to toy with her, she reached behind her back and unclasped the bra, removing it and tossing it in the floor.

Sighing just a little, he realized he had missed those, too. Leaning forward, he caught her right nipple in his mouth and began to tease it with his tongue.

She only let him continue to taste her for another minute, then she pulled back and said, "Wait, I want to try something."

Withdrawing his fingers from between her legs, he watched as she climbed off the couch and into the floor, getting down on her knees. Then she went for his jeans, tugging them and the underwear beneath them down to his ankles.

His cock was happy to have its freedom, and even happier when she curled her fingers around it and shoved her hair back over her shoulder. It became ecstatic when she bent and took the tip in her mouth, a bit tentatively at first, but then she pulled back, licked her lips, and slid her mouth over half of his length.

"Oh, fuck," he ground out as she took more of him into her mouth, finally easing down until he could feel his cock at the back of her throat.

Willow moaned, moving slowly at first, but before long she was picking up the pace. She actually seemed enthusiastic, and much faster than he was used to, he felt his climax approaching. He reached down and placed a hand on her shoulder to warn her, and she sped up even more. And then he was coming, one hand tightening on her shoulder, the other gripping the couch cushion, and she kept her mouth around him, taking every last bit.

While he rested against the back of the couch to recover, Willow pulled the top of her dress back on and zipped it up, leaving her bra in the floor. Then she got on the couch, curling her legs up beneath her, and rested her head on his shoulder.

"I wouldn't have taken you for a swallower," he stated, reaching over to take her hand.

She gave his hand a little squeeze and said, "Spitting isn't ladylike."

He choked on a burst of laughter. "I've never heard that before."

"Well, now you know," she replied easily.

Regaining some of his strength, he leaned forward and tilted his head so he could place a little kiss on top of her head. "Thank you."

She made an affirmative noise and they stayed just like that for a few minutes, no words, just companionable silence and cuddling.

Finally, she said she would be right back and headed to the bathroom, so he took the opportunity to get himself fully dressed again.

Of all the possibilities he had thought of on his way over, *that* had not been one of them. In dreams a couple times, but definitely not in real life.

When Willow emerged, she stopped behind the couch, placing a hand on his shoulder and telling him she would be back, she needed to go check on dinner.

Instead of waiting for her by himself in the living room, he grabbed the wine he had brought and followed her.

"Do you want me to help with anything?" he asked.

"Can you cook?" she asked, glancing over her shoulder as she filled a pot with water.

"Of course I can cook. I mean, not *foie gras* or anything, but I can cook regular stuff."

Willow shook her head. "Thank you anyway. You can get out the wine glasses if you want," she said, indicating the cupboard.

It wasn't much, but he grabbed the wine glasses and took them over to the table, which she had already set prior to his arrival. There was already an empty glass for each of them, and she even set up a candle in the center of the table nearest their spots. That made him smile a little.

"So, which one of your boyfriends was going to be the lucky date if I would've been busy?" he asked, leaning against the counter and crossing his arms as he watched her put a lid on the pot she had just placed on the stove.

Adjusting the heat, she turned around and smiled. "Why? Jealous?"

"No. Well… maybe if he was also going to get dessert first…"

Willow grinned, but didn't confirm or deny it. "My reserve tonight was actually my ex-boyfriend. I should probably text him, come to think of it," she said, walking to the other end of the counter to find her phone.

"The one you dumped?" he asked, frowning slightly.

"Uh, no, not that one," she said as her thumbs flew rapidly across the screen. "My ex-boyfriend before him— Caden. He was the big brother of one of my girlfriends, but I don't really talk to her much anymore."

He wasn't sure if he should appreciate the ease with which she seemed to switch between guys, or be a little insulted by it. "So the dress wasn't specifically for me then?"

Apparently finished texting, she put her phone down and shoved it to the back of the counter, returning her attention to him with a smile. "No, the dress was for you. I was wearing jeans earlier."

"What about panties?"

Her grin widened. "I was wearing panties earlier, too."

Ethan shook his head in amusement. "You've never been dumped before, have you?"

"I have. Actually Caden dumped me—part of why he doesn't get the dress," she informed him with a wink.

"I don't know that I deserve the dress either, to be honest."

Willow merely shrugged. "We don't get what we deserve out of life, Ethan."

That little nugget of truth wiped the smile right off his face, but she just turned around, reaching into a cabinet above her head and pulling down two shallow bowls.

"Do you want bread with your salad?"

He watched as she pulled a giant loaf of bread out of its brown paper sleeve, placing it on top of the cutting board and reaching for a large knife.

"Uh, yeah, I'll have a piece."

She nodded and sliced off two pieces of bread, placing one on the edge of each shallow bowl and moving the knife to the sink.

With the knife safely out of reach, he walked up behind her and slowly moved his arms around her waist. She tensed initially, but then she relaxed and leaned back against him, resting her hands on top of his.

"Can I ask you a question?" Ethan asked.

"Of course."

"Are you having bad dreams again?"

Her shoulders tensed and she stepped out of his embrace, flashing an irritated glance at him over her shoulder as she took the bowls to the table. "I don't want to talk about that."

"Why didn't you tell me?" he asked, taking her response as verification that she was.

She shook her head, but didn't bother responding. Instead, she moved on to the next task, taking the bowl of salad she had already prepared out of the fridge and placing it in the center of the table.

"If you want tomatoes or cucumbers in your salad, just let me know and I can chop some up for you."

"I don't care about tomatoes, Willow," he said, catching her by the shoulder and turning her to look at him.

Sure enough, beneath the make-up she had attempted to cover them up with, there were dark smudges under her eyes.

Ethan sighed. "I thought...I thought they stopped."

"They did. For a while. Then they came back." She shrugged, averting her gaze. "It didn't work. Oh well."

"I'm sorry," he told her.

"It's not your fault," she told him, breaking free and resuming her busy work. "It was a valiant effort."

"When did they start up again?"

"Does it matter?" Willow replied. "I'm working on a new theory of getting rid of them, but it's trial and error at this point."

"Are you still seeing your counselor?" Ethan inquired.

"Yep. Haven't told her everything though—I kind of thought she might not understand."

"Well…she is *trained* to better understand these kinds of things, Willow."

Pausing to spare him a look of disbelief, she said, "Really? You think she would understand *this*? I don't think *this* is normal. Maybe I'm wrong, but I'm fairly confident that I'm not."

Since he didn't know how to argue with that, he let it go for the moment.

By the time they sat down to dinner, he seemed to have succeeded in lowering her guard again. He was still a little pissed at himself for not noticing earlier, and he couldn't understand why she wouldn't just open up instead of making him pry every little thing out of her. It would be so much easier—but then, that was probably just part of what made her Willow, the beguiling creature that she was.

# CHAPTER NINETEEN

"That was amazing."

Willow offered a smile as Ethan helped her clear the table. "I'm glad you enjoyed it."

The food had been delicious, the wine had helped ease what little tension had remained, and after only one glass, Willow's cheeks had pinkened and she was even more pleasant than usual.

But dinner was over.

Ethan wasn't immediately sure where to go from there. They were still in the kitchen, and he checked his watch, asking, "Do you know what time your parents will be home?"

"Not precisely, but I know they'll still be out for a little while." Approaching him and reaching for his hand, she asked, "Do you want to go to my room?"

Of course he did, even if he was a bit conflicted about it.

After a quick stop in the living room to retrieve her bra, Willow led Ethan upstairs and down the hall into her bedroom.

Once inside, he was momentarily distracted by the girlish hues. Her walls were painted lavender with a couple of abstract canvas paintings on opposite walls, the carpet was plushy and white, and her bedspread was black and white with the names of several international cities printed on it—Paris, Rome, New York, etc. There were decorative pillows set up, some matching the bedspread, some that matched the walls, and a few that matched both to pull the look together.

Her dresser was white with a mirror behind it, against the wall by the door he suspected was either a closet or a bathroom. Atop the dresser, a couple of framed pictures of her and her friends, a blue candle in a glass jar, a small stack of magazines, and several bottles of nail polish.

Once more, he was reminded of her age. It was easy to forget when he was alone with her—too easy.

As if sensing that he was about to have a crisis of conscience, Willow came up behind him and wrapped her arms around his waist, just like he had done in the kitchen earlier.

"Don't judge me by the teenage girl paraphernalia that's scattered around my room," she said lightly.

Cracking a smile, he said, "Did a teenage girl sneak in here and plant it so I'd find it?"

"Yes," she enthused. "She's such a bitch. I keep trying to get rid of her but the garlic necklace and salt circle were both a bust."

Ethan shook his head. "You should really have someone take care of that. What would your army of boyfriends think?"

"They're teenage boys, so I highly doubt they would find it so offensive," she pointed out. Tugging on his arm, she prompted him to turn around. He did, wrapping his arms around her waist, looking down at her.

"You're trouble, you know that?" he asked.

Willow shook her head. "I'm sweet as pie, I don't know what you're talking about."

Despite his sigh, his hand moved to her face and he ran the backs of his fingers along her jaw before cupping her face in his hand. Willow leaned into it and closed her eyes, so open to his touch.

"I don't understand you," he murmured, pulling her closer so he could place a kiss on her forehead.

"What don't you understand?"

Sighing, Ethan said, "I'm not trying to bullshit you or anything , but I don't think it's a stretch to say you could pretty much have your pick of guys. Why am *I* here?"

Instead of feigning modesty and denying it, or even smiling and teasing him about it, her lips pressed together and she seemed to contemplate her response. After a minute, she came up with one. "I could be here with someone else, sure, but…I feel like it needs to be you. I can't compartmentalize you the way that I would need to in order to file you away— you're in too many different compartments. We've blurred— *I've* blurred the lines in such a way that…" She trailed off, uncertain how to explain it. Her brow furrowed.

"You certainly haven't blurred the lines on your own, Willow," he told her, shaking his head slightly. "That's as much my fault—*more* my fault than it is yours."

Her gray eyes shot to his, a little frustrated. "It's not about fault. I'm not trying to place blame on anyone. I just…I need to try to make a new memory. You'll always be my first, whether you think I should think of it that way or not, it doesn't change the facts. You *were* the first, maybe not the first that I picked, but the first all the same. Maybe my feelings for you have changed since then—I haven't daydreamed about a fiery spike piercing your torso recently— but that just makes the memories…weirder. It's like when you go to sleep and dream your significant other is cheating on you and you wake up angry at them, even though they didn't actually do anything—only, instead of that, it's…ripping away my virginity in front of a group of criminals, a couple of whom are clearly planning to do the same fucking thing to me at the next available opportunity. I'm not your high school girlfriend, I didn't expect candles, but…my expectations were a little bit more than what I got."

Just hearing her reiterate the gory details caused Ethan's stomach to sink. Images flung themselves to the forefront of his mind—Lane with the gun to her head, the bloody condom, Willow curled up on the ground, crying. His stomach rolled over.

There was nothing he could say or do to make up for it, and he hated being reminded of that. "I'm sorr—"

Willow placed her hand over his mouth, shaking her head. "You don't have to apologize again. I wasn't trying to make you feel bad, just trying to answer your question."

Before he could argue, Willow stood on her tiptoes, looping her arm around his neck, and tugged him down to kiss her.

Slow at first, Willow escalated things when she caught his lower lips between her teeth and tugged, then slipped her tongue into his mouth and surprised him with her aggression.

Ethan could feel his own desire stirring as he tugged her closer, matching her eagerness. He slowly walked her backward until the backs of her legs hit the bed, skimming her curves with his fingertips, then placing his hands under her ass and lifting her. She wrapped her legs around him instinctively and a minute later they were on the bed, and he was tossing those damn decorative pillows on the floor as Willow scooted backward, trying not to break their kiss.

Finally she did break the kiss, needing air, but he took the opportunity to start kissing his way up her neck, which made Willow moan—which in turn, drove him crazy.

"Are you sure you want to do this?" he murmured, wanting to stop then if she was going to change her mind.

"Mm hmm," she murmured back, her fingers delving through his hair, the other hand resting on his back, holding his body close to hers.

He hoped to hell she was sure. Stopping in the hotel room had been hard, and he wasn't eager to do that again.

"I want to ask you something that may sound kind of weird," Willow said.

Ethan pulled back to look at her, but she wasn't looking in his eyes, focusing instead on his chest.

"Okay?"

"I want you to—to fuck me really hard, okay?"

His cock stirred, but Ethan still had the presence of mind to hesitate. "I mean, it's your first time, so I should probably...go easy on you, you know? Your body isn't going to—"

"I'll listen to my body," she interrupted. "That's what I want. If I can't handle it and I change my mind, I'll tell you. I trust you to stop and change gears."

He swallowed, studying her, but she still wouldn't look at him. Feeling uneasy about the whole situation, Ethan said, "I don't think this is a good idea, Willow. This isn't how your first time should be...."

Ignoring his concerns, her hand drifted down his chest, over his stomach, and she lightly rubbed between his legs. "I'm gonna need a better reason than that," she murmured.

"You should be with someone else," he said roughly. "Someone younger, someone better."

"I assure you I'm old enough to decide for myself who I'm interested in," she replied, running her fingers lightly down his chest, the other hand still between his legs. "But thanks for your concern."

"I'm not right for you," he told her.

He wasn't wrong. She just didn't care.

"I don't want to be with anyone else," she stated.

For a moment, he looked like he was going to argue, but then his hand was searching behind her back for the zipper, and Willow rolled over, giving him better access. A bit more slowly than she expected, he tugged the zipper down her back, over the curve of her ass, all the way to the bottom, his fingers surprising her as he used his other hand to lightly trail his fingers up and down the backs of her thighs.

Since she was on her stomach and he was behind her, she couldn't see him, but when his fingers reached the apex of her thighs, she spread her legs slightly, and took a rapid breath when he slid a finger inside of her. She was already wet, so he met with no resistance, and even though she had wanted to be able to see him the whole time, it didn't seem to bother her that she couldn't.

The bed creaked as he moved onto it, keeping the hand between her legs and crawling closer.

"What do *you* like?" he asked, using his free hand to brush her long hair across the shoulder opposite the side he was on.

"I don't know," she said shyly—even if it seemed a little silly to be shy when he had a finger inside of her and she was lying pretty much naked on her bed beside him.

"Did you like when I ate your pussy?"

Inhaling sharply in surprise, she chuckled a bit weakly and felt her face turning red. She hadn't expected him to *mention* it—and she expected to be excited by hearing him say it even less.

"Hmm?"

"Yes."

"Would you like me to do that again?"

Biting down on her lip, she momentarily debated. That was a hard no, but it wasn't her end goal for the night. Allowing just a hint of her dissatisfaction to come through—

playfully, of course—she glanced at him and responded wryly, "No, I want you to fuck me, not just get me off."

"Who says we can't do both?" he replied, lifting an eyebrow.

"Apparently you." She lifted her own eyebrows.

He gave her a dry glare and pushed a second finger inside of her. Then, leaning in and placing a little kiss on her shoulder, he gave her a devilish grin. "I promise to fuck you as thoroughly as you want me to."

With that proclamation, he withdrew his fingers from between her legs and rolled her over, peeling the dress off the bed and tossing it in the floor.

She pushed herself up with one arm and lifted an eyebrow. "You're wearing an awful lot of clothes for someone who's about to fuck me."

He grinned, not needing further encouragement, and tugged his sweater over his head. Another damn undershirt, but he made quick work of removing that as well, then he was just in his jeans. He didn't take those off though. Instead, he got off the bed and said, "If at any point you don't like what I'm doing, even a little, just tell me so, okay?"

Willow bobbed her head. "I will."

He began unbuttoning and unzipping his jeans and Willow pushed herself up into a sitting position, a bit uncertain, a touch self-conscious.

Her mind started to drift backwards as she considered him looking at her naked, since it was hardly the first time, but she hit the brakes and forced herself to stay in the present.

Once undressed, Ethan took a step closer to the edge of the bed, but didn't climb back on it. Instead he leaned forward, reaching a hand out to Willow.

Climbing to her knees, she inched closer to the edge of the bed until she was leaning against his body for support. Her arms wound naturally around his neck and she smiled as his hands came to rest on her waist.

Ethan pulled back a little, his gaze roaming down over her naked body, his mouth slowly curving up in an appreciative smile.

"You're beautiful, you know that?"

Glowing a bit, she met his eyes playfully. "I wouldn't kick you out of bed, either."

He rolled his eyes with a grin, pulling her close again so that she was pressed up against his hard body. "Stop, I'm blushing," he teased.

She opened her mouth to retort, but he cut her off with a kiss. It was gentle at first, comfortable and sweet, but as soon as she felt herself relaxing against him and he noticed her pliancy, the kiss grew in ferocity—became rougher, more demanding. Quick and hot, not letting her catch her breath as his hands roamed over her body, setting her skin on fire everywhere that he touched her. When he kissed her like that, she felt almost woozy with pleasure. She'd never felt that way when anyone else kissed her.

Her body strained to get closer to him, but they were already skin-to-skin—it wasn't enough. She felt feverish, her hands drifting over his powerful shoulders, squeezing, then running up and down his muscular back.

"I want you," she murmured when he finally broke the kiss, her head falling languidly to the side so his lips had no trouble finding her neck.

His fingers dug into her hips and excitement coursed through her body—it was confirmation enough that he felt the same way.

His hands left her hips and she felt momentarily abandoned—but then his strong hands were framing her face, and he was looking at her so tenderly that she nearly melted into a puddle, right there on her bed.

He really needed to not do that.

Her heart felt vaguely achy as he leaned in and kissed her again, that time gentler, but somehow just as intoxicating.

*Please don't make me fall in love with you,* she thought, for the first time *really* wondering if she was making a huge mistake.

It was too late though, she knew that. The magic he worked on her with only his mouth made her dizzy, and the curiosity of what it could be like between them—like this—was too tempting to resist.

Her pulse was skittering, and she felt drunk—it had nothing to do with the glass of wine she had with dinner and everything to do with the man kissing her literally senseless. When one of his hands dropped from her face and lightly trailed up the inside of her thigh, she sighed into the kiss, the muscles between her legs tensing in anticipation. Instead of delving between her legs, he teased her, coming close and then stopping and drifting down the other leg. It was pure torture—he was driving her crazy.

The bastard knew it, too. He smiled into the kiss, and just for that, she bit his lip. At that, he growled and gave her what she wanted, plunging a finger between her legs…but it wasn't enough. It felt like he was still teasing her. She wanted more. She wanted *him.*

"You know, if you're game, we can skip the foreplay," she told him.

"Mm, eager for me, are you?"

Reaching down between his legs, she wrapped her hand around his thick cock and said, "I don't think I'm alone there."

Ethan offered a strained smile and reached down to guide her hand away. "All right, let me grab a condom."

Pointing directly to her right, she said, "Nightstand."

Lifting an eyebrow, he said, "Damn, you came prepared."

Giving him a little wink, she inched backward so she didn't fall off the bed when he took a step closer to the nightstand, grabbing one of the colorful foil packets.

Tossing a glance back at her, he said, "I think you might be overestimating my stamina though—six condoms?"

"There were different kinds, I didn't know which ones you liked," she said with a shrug. "Not like I could text you and ask."

"I bet you got some funny looks at the checkout," he remarked, ripping open the packet and discarding it on the nightstand as he used his other hand to roll the condom down over himself.

"It was a young guy, he was basically as red as a fire engine the whole time he rung me out."

Smirking as he approached the bed, Ethan remarked, "I bet he was pretty jealous."

"Of the army of men I was clearly planning on banging? Obviously," she said, rolling her eyes jokingly.

Narrowing his eyes as he reached out and tugged her legs straight, he grasped her just above the ankles and pulled her down until her ass was near the edge of the bed. "You won't be thinking about your army of boyfriends tonight, I promise you that."

It shouldn't please her so much to poke at his possessive side—especially since he shouldn't even have one where she was concerned, but maybe that was why it thrilled her.

Not that they were lacking in forbidden elements in their relationship, she acknowledged dryly.

Then he pulled her legs open and stepped forward, and all remnants of humor fled her mind, replaced momentarily with a sort of final panic. It was about to happen, and her heart was suddenly pounding, her chest tightening.

Ethan paused. Her sudden apprehension must have been showing on her face, because his touch gentled, the hands on her ankles moved up her legs to her thighs, and then he knelt down and placed a kiss on the inside of her thigh, just above the kneecap. Then, slowly, still touching her with just the tips of his fingers, he trailed the kisses up the inside of her thigh, and the *good* tension in her lower abdomen began to build again. His tongue darted out, just barely touching her skin and she gasped, bracing her hands on the bed.

"You like that?" he asked warmly, his velvety voice further soothing her nerves.

"Yes," she said on a sigh.

After making his way up every inch of the inside of her thigh, his face was finally between her legs, and she could feel the pulsing there, simultaneously wanting another taste of that pleasure she had felt in the hotel room, and wanting him to stop and bury himself inside of her.

"I'm ready," she told him.

"You sure?"

She nodded, and he must have believed her because he straightened, then he reached for her hips, lifting them off the bed and pulling her closer to his arousal.

It was impossible not to tense, even if she wanted him all the way down to her core, and then she felt the tip of him push just inside of her and she took a deep breath, fisting her hands at her sides.

Ethan was watching her face, but the apprehension must have looked less like horror that time because he didn't stop. With one of his thumbs, he lightly rubbed her hip, almost reassuringly.

"You have no idea how long I've wanted to be inside of you," he told her, pushing just another inch.

Willow couldn't help smiling a little at that. "Could've fooled me."

Ethan managed a smile, but it looked strained. Then, without further ado, he pushed forward, pushing his whole length inside of her.

It felt almost like relief to Willow. He stayed like that for a moment, letting her body (and maybe her mind) adjust to the invasion.

It was only uncomfortable for a few seconds, then she began to relax, and the fullness inside of her felt less like an invasion, because it was welcome.

After half a minute passed, Willow nodded to let him know she was good.

Still gripping her by the hips, he slowly pulled out of her, then he pushed back in, and the passage went much smoother that time—still tight, but not uncomfortable.

He made a hissing sound as he surged forward the third time, and the look of pleasure on his face fed *her* pleasure.

"I want you to kiss me," she said.

He opened his eyes and looked down at her. Then he nodded, pulling out again, and telling her to move to a different spot on the bed.

After he finished repositioning them, he was on the bed with Willow straddling him. At first she wasn't sure about the position, but as she lowered herself onto his cock and she saw the tension on his face, she realized she felt more powerful in that position—and she didn't hate it.

Lifting herself slowly up and down the length of him, not only did it feel really damn good for her, but Ethan finally seemed to be feeling some of her earlier frustration. When she continued the movement but leaned in to kiss him, his mouth crushed against hers hungrily and fire shot through her veins. He didn't normally seem to be as intensely affected by their kisses, but that time he was—his hands were everywhere, on her breasts, running down her sides, digging into her hips, nearly scoring her back with his nails, but he caught himself before he did and it became a tender caress. Coupled with kissing her like his life depended on it, that fed her own appetite and she sped up, desperate for more friction, wanting everything to be harder and faster, as frantic as the feelings twisting up inside of her.

After a few minutes he stopped her, flipping her onto her back and thrusting inside of her as soon as he could get between her legs. She moaned, closing her eyes for just a moment, relishing the feeling of his whole length inside of her. Then he was pulling out again, establishing a rhythm, but he quickly abandoned it in favor of faster and harder thrusts. Finally he was fucking her so hard, fingers digging into the sides of her thighs, that the bed was moving in time with his thrusts. The pressure inside of her was unbearable, and she wanted to beg for more, but just for the sake of begging—he was already giving her what she was craving.

"Harder, Ethan," she all but growled, raking her nails down his back.

He threw his head back, closing his eyes and uttering a strained, "Oh, fuck me."

Willow grinned, feeling a little satisfied with herself, but then somehow he picked up the pace and took her harder, and the feeling that she was about to lose her mind intensified—but the promise of going over the brink was so goddamn delicious, she didn't even care.

And then she felt it, her muscles convulsing around his cock as her head fell back and she cried out loudly, ecstasy exploding in every one of her nerve endings.

Her body trembled as she went limp. He was still moving between her legs, and she tried to muster the strength to contribute, but before she had to, his body went rigid and he released a groan, burying himself as deep inside of her as he could and reaching his own climax.

At least she remembered to flex her muscles a bit, and he groaned again, a jagged little groan, moving inside of her just slightly.

Then he collapsed on top of her, as spent as she was, and she smiled dazedly, wrapping her arms around him, loving everything about the moment—his weight against her, the feeling of him still inside of her, and the overwhelming sense of satisfaction and peace that seemed to envelop her.

Everything was perfect, at least for that moment.

Closing her eyes, she wished that perfect moment could go on forever.

# CHAPTER TWENTY

Ethan must have nodded off for a few minutes, but when he woke up, he was momentarily surprised to find a naked woman in his arms.

Willow tilted her head back to look at him and she smiled faintly. "There you are. I wasn't going to let you sleep much longer."

"Sorry. How long was I out?"

"Not long, maybe ten minutes."

Oh good. No hurry then.

He sighed, wrapping both arms around her and lightly squeezing her. She happily squeezed him right back, tenderly brushing her lips across his chest.

"That was nice," she informed him.

"Yes, it was," he agreed, tucking a fallen lock of hair behind her ear. "Very nice."

Leaving several more kisses across his chest, she paused when she got to a nipple, then she took it between her teeth and bit down.

Growling a little, Ethan tugged her up closer to his face. "If you keep that up, I'm going to want an encore performance."

She grinned at him, resting her arms on his chest, then resting her chin on her arms and looked up at him. "You say that like it's a bad thing. We have *a lot* of condoms, so...."

Ethan shook his head, but smiled indulgently. "You...I don't know what to make of you, I swear."

"You know, we *could* take a shower before you have to go. We might even be able to squeeze in that encore round," she suggested.

Sighing, he replied, "You would tease me with shower sex."

"Nope, not teasing. Totally willing to follow through." She pointed to the door past her dresser. "Shower's right in there, I'm ready when you are."

Lightly brushing his thumb across her cheek, he said, "As much as I love you for offering—" He stopped, realizing what he said. "I meant—"

"I know what you meant," she interrupted. "Proceed."

"I can't go home with wet hair, smelling like soap or shampoo that we don't use."

"Ah," she said, nodding a little. "I hadn't considered that." Then she shrugged, moving off of his chest and curling up in the crook of his arm. "Oh well, I offered."

"Sorry," he murmured.

She shrugged a little, resting one of her hands on his chest. "Can I ask you something? I don't want to make you mad though, I'm not judging or anything."

His gaze dropped to her shoulder, and he began lightly dragging his finger in little circles on her upper arm. "Sure."

"Do you feel guilty, being here like this, with me?"

Smiling a little dryly, he said, "When I think about it."

Dipping her head, she murmured, "Sorry."

"It's okay," he said easily. Then, since it hadn't been a very satisfying answer, he added, "I don't think of this as...cheating. That's probably my own fucked up way of rationalizing, but when I'm here, with you, I don't feel like...I feel like our past, our relationship is separate. It's this whole life that Amanda knows nothing about, a life separate from her. Regular rules don't apply right here, right now. If they did, I wouldn't be here."

"Men are better compartmentalizers than women. I read that somewhere once, I don't remember where. Have you ever cheated on Amanda before?"

"No."

"Ever thought about it?"

"Once," he answered honestly. "Marriage isn't easy all the time. It's a lot of work. It wears on you after a while."

"You don't have to make excuses, I just wondered."

"I don't have to make excuses, I didn't act on it, I was just explaining. You're young, you haven't been in any relationship long enough for it to become difficult, burdened by the stressful situations that everyday life can throw at you. You haven't been with someone long enough for the romance to become stale, stagnant to the point that you don't even feel like lovers anymore, on any level."

"I didn't say I had," she replied easily.

He realized he was being defensive so he stopped. "Have you ever cheated on a boyfriend?"

"No. If I don't want to be with him anymore, I leave."

Ethan smiled slightly. "Smart."

"Yep," she replied, nodding her head. "I'm not like a lot of other girls; I have an odd way about me when it comes to relationships—I did even before all of this happened, and I doubt this is going to make things any easier."

"Knowing when to get out isn't a bad thing. It's far more common for young women to tolerate a lot of shit they shouldn't until they're in over their heads."

Grinning, Willow looked at up him. "Don't say young women, it makes you sound old."

"Wait until you hear me telling all the kids to get off my lawn."

"Mm, sexy," she teased.

He let the moment pass, then he said, "I'm a little surprised you're putting up with this, considering."

"You haven't surpassed my bullshit tolerance level. Plus... I like you. I like the way you're honest, I like how you make me feel most of the time. I like that you know you're not a good guy and you're not a bad guy, because that's how most people are, they just don't have the guts to admit it. I like your flaws."

"I would say I like your flaws, too, but honestly I've seen very few."

Smiling and biting her lip, she asked, "Which ones have you noticed?"

"Aw, no, you can't ask that when we're in bed together. I do have manners. For tonight, you're perfect."

Willow wrinkled up her nose. "No, that would be fake. Nobody's perfect. I would hate it if you thought I was."

He tugged her a little closer. "You're pretty great though, you know that, right?"

"Of course," she said playfully. "Just ask my army of boyfriends."

He squeezed her and she laughed. "I get jealous occasionally," he admitted.

"I know," she replied, sounding amused.

"I have no right to."

"I know that, too. I don't mind though. It's cute."

"Cute?" he asked, laughing lightly.

She merely nodded, wrapping her arms around him more snugly. "In moderation, it's cute. I do too, once in a great while. That's new for me. I don't usually get jealous. Then again, my usual companions aren't married, and if they were, I doubt they would tell me about date nights with their wives."

Ethan grimaced, remembering that cringe-worthy text. "That was probably rude."

Willow just shrugged. "I guess it was just honest. Maybe too honest though—I think there's typically a don't-ask-don't-tell policy in situations like this."

"Sorry."

She didn't seem overly concerned, so he let the topic drop.

For a moment, he just enjoyed holding her, enjoyed the feeling of her arms wrapped around him—enjoyed that moment, separate from his own life.

He wondered if her attempt to replace the first experience would work even a little bit.

Where would they go from there? In a way, it seemed like the completion of their time together—like closure. They had begun their journey in that fucked up place and shattered everything, and he felt like they had exhausted their last effort to try to heal those wounds. The line was beginning to blur already—he hadn't thought of it as an affair before, but lying in her bed with her naked body pressed up against his, he couldn't think of another word for it. Not anymore. Before, he could pretend he was only trying to help her.

Fucking her was not helping her.

Even admitting that, he couldn't bring himself to regret it. Not yet.

"What do you want out of life?" he found himself asking her.

A few seconds passed, then she said, "The same thing most people want, I guess. To be happy, loved, fulfilled. I want to travel and see new places, experience new things. Live out my dreams."

"What are your dreams? What do you want to do after college?"

"Honestly? I'd like to have my own art gallery."

Quirking an eyebrow, he said, "Really? I never knew you liked art. What do you like about it?"

"Well, we haven't exactly talked about it," she pointed out. "I like how it's open to interpretation—the same piece can mean a million different things to a million different people. I seldom see anything the way other people do; at least in the art world, that's perfectly acceptable. Do you have any interest?"

"I never studied it much. I think the extent of my exposure was the humanities class in college—Botticelli, Da Vinci, Van Gogh, Michelangelo, those guys."

"That makes sense. I want to go to Italy one of these days, see the Sistine Chapel. And Paris. I want to go everywhere. Well, not *everywhere*, but at least a lot of places."

He smiled absently. "I hope you do."

"If that doesn't work out, then maybe open my own restaurant. I want to work for myself, regardless, not for someone else."

"I can understand that. I always felt that way, too."

"What about you?" Willow asked, tilting her head back to look up at him. "What did you want to do with your life?"

"I'm doing what I wanted to do. Professionally, anyway. I wanted to be a detective initially, but then I realized I didn't actually want to get into law enforcement." Ethan shook his head slightly. "I was angry when I was your age. I wasn't focused on where I was going or what I was doing with my life, I was just concentrating on getting out, getting away as fast and as far as I could. You seem much more put together than I was."

"Try telling my parents that," she joked.

"They don't think you've got it together?"

"Not anymore. They don't understand that I'm not the same as I was before, and I don't understand either...but I'm not. I'm just not the same. I used to be more normal than this," she told him, tilting her head back to look up at him.

He smiled faintly, his fingers still caressing her bare shoulder. "Yeah, me too."

She nodded in understanding. "Why were you so angry?"

"Crappy childhood. The usual," he said lightly.

She nodded, not prying since he didn't seem to want to go into detail. "What about personally? Did you always want to get married and have kids?"

"Yeah, eventually. I always thought I would've waited a little longer than I did, but I always wanted kids." He smiled a little. "I know you're at a different stage in your life, but you'll see if you have kids someday. They're like nothing else. Being a parent is...it's really great."

"I think I want kids someday," she told him. "Or at least one. I'm not firm on a number. Not like 12 or anything, but 1 or 2. Step kids are fine, too. Obviously if I end up with my professor, at his age, there could be step kids involved," she added lightly.

Ethan cracked a smile. "Obviously. Do you want to get married?"

"Maybe. It's interesting that you ask that, most people assume marriage is a given if you want kids."

"Your parents aren't married," he pointed out.

"That's true, but that's a little different, isn't it?"

"I guess. Not completely. You can build a life with someone without being married. I don't have to tell you that. The state of marriage is really just a piece of paper, in the scheme of things."

Smiling slightly, she said, "I take it your wife was the one who wanted to get married?"

"It was mutual, but yeah, she was pushing for it more than I was. I wasn't in a hurry, but I'm not anti-marriage or anything. I just don't think it's necessary."

"I agree," she said. "It's not something that's ever been important to me. I'm definitely not the girl who's been planning her wedding since she was 12."

"You will never inspire your own romantic comedy."

Cracking a grin, she said, "Damn, there goes that life goal."

A moment of companionable silence passed, and Ethan thought about checking the time, but…he wasn't ready to give up the night just yet.

"Tell me something else, something about you."

"Like what?" she asked.

"I don't know, anything. Tell me about your family or your fears."

"Mm, well, my fears have been updated and would only taint the moment, so we'll go with my family. You've met most of them, so you have a pretty good idea already. I have two moms and a brother, my mom is the optimistic one, forever seeing the glass half full. Even if you tell her straight, 'Mom, this damn glass is empty' she will be disheartened for however long, then she will repress the knowledge again and literally forget that you ever told her. Ashlynn had a rough start in life, and kind of a rough middle, too. I don't know anything about her family really, because she doesn't talk to them. She and my mom have been together since I was four, and my brother is two years younger than me. He's…pretty much your average teenage boy, but he's always there for me when I need him to be."

"What about your dad?"

"Yeah, he's not so much my dad as just some guy that my mom slept with because she was young and stupid and thought he was exciting, and then—whoops—I was born. Now we all have to deal with it."

"You're not close at all?"

She scoffed. "If by close you mean he didn't even care that I was kidnapped, then yeah, we're tight."

"You never heard from him at all?" Ethan asked, frowning.

"He sent me flowers and a stupid gift card," she said with annoyance. "He didn't even call right away. Even when he does try to call now, it's like…I just don't even want to talk to him. His actions have said plenty since everything happened. I mean, I didn't expect him to become Liam Neeson or anything, but…I did expect *some* concern."

"That's crazy. I can't even imagine that."

Willow nodded. "He won't be winning father of the year anytime soon—at least, not from me. Who knows how he is with his other kids."

"Do you know any of his other kids?"

Shaking her head, she said, "Not really. I've met them a few times—the legitimate ones, at least; if he has more bastards, I've never met them—but we don't talk or anything. I barely talk to *him,* so…"

"That sucks, I'm sorry."

"I'm better off. Honestly, I've finally lost the desire after all this. He called yesterday and I didn't even call him back. I used to…pathetically crave his approval," she said, rolling her eyes. "It was a fool's errand, and I hated that I even cared, so I guess I should be glad that he gave me the push I needed."

"It's not pathetic, it's normal, but I know what you mean."

Suddenly, startling them both, Ethan's phone vibrated on the bedside table. Neither of them expected the interruption, so both of their gazes jerked to the screen.

A photo flashed across the screen, maybe a text message, and Ethan grabbed for the phone, but before he could tilt it away from her, she got a good view of an adorable baby in a blue and white blanket sleeper, conked out in a bed, his little mouth gaping open, his head tilted back, and an empty pillow on the side of the bed behind him.

A pained expression flashed across Ethan's face and he looked at it briefly before closing the message and pushing himself up into a sitting position.

Willow moved off of him, and he sat on the edge of the bed, scratching the back of his neck and not looking at her. "I have to go."

"Okay," she said, a bit weakly.

Bending to grab his discarded clothes off the floor, he quickly pulled his underwear and pants back on, then glanced back at her. "I'm sorry."

Forcing a smile, she shrugged her shoulders. "It's okay."

He opened his mouth like he wanted to say something else, but then he closed it and pulled his sweater over his head.

Willow didn't know what to say either. The very moment she wanted to go on forever only a minute ago was suddenly lasting forever, and it felt like a punishment.

She couldn't even seem to make herself get up off the bed. Instead, she yanked the blanket up to cover herself, frowning a little at the change in atmosphere.

Ethan slipped his phone back into his pocket. "Um…"

"Do you mind just locking up? I…I think I'm gonna take that shower, so…"

"Sure," he said, nodding briefly. Then, almost hesitantly, he said, "The…wine bottle. Your parents might notice that wasn't here before."

"You can take it, or just throw it out. Or I'll just say Caden brought it over."

"Right." He nodded once more, hesitating as he made his way to the door.

It looked like he wanted to say something else, and she sort of wanted him to, but nothing came.

"I'll text you," he finally said.

Smiling thinly, Willow nodded. "Okay."

And then he was gone.

Shoulders slumping, instead of going in to take her shower, Willow climbed under the blankets, pulling them up around her, and hugged the pillow that still smelled like him.

# CHAPTER TWENTY ONE

From the time he pulled out of Willow's driveway, large chunks of Ethan's waking hours were devoted to trying to decide what to say next time he spoke to her.

He wanted to tell her that their situation could only end badly. That he felt like a bastard for letting it happen, for putting her in that position in the first place, but as much as it would suck for both of them, it would be easiest in the long run if they cut things off sooner, rather than later. Not only because he knew for a fact that the longer an affair went on, the higher the chances of getting caught, but because he didn't want to hurt her more than he was already going to.

He also didn't want to say that and sound like an asshole, since Willow often seemed very casual, and maybe it wouldn't hurt her as much as he thought it would. Maybe she would brush it off, replace him with any number of guys who would be happy to fill his spot, and go on about her life without concern.

Even if he selfishly disliked the idea of being so replaceable, that was what he was hoping for. Everything he had seen so far indicated that might be the case... everything except the look on her face when he got that text from Amanda.

He couldn't believe he forgot to shut his damn phone off.

When Amanda sent him the text about Caleb having a fever, he was glad that he hadn't, at least after the awkwardness with Willow. It wasn't like she didn't know he had a wife and kids at home, but knowing that and seeing evidence of it were two different things.

By morning, Caleb's fever had dissipated without explanation. Amanda took him to the doctor anyway just to make sure, and everything checked out.

Ethan felt like the worst person ever.

Torn between Amanda, who was patient enough to give him the space he'd been needing since he came back home, and Willow, who forgave him for hurting her and then invited him to hurt her some more.

He should have known better. *Did* know better.

Dammit.

How could he have let that happen?

How could he stop it, without making more of a mess?

When he was with Willow it *felt* like a separate life, but he didn't have two lives, he only had one.

And she didn't fit into it.

But he wanted her to.

Even if he knew logically that the only sane course of action was cutting her loose, he knew right down to bottom of his soul that he would miss her.

He should have never slept with her. It was a line that he knew better than to cross, and yet, he did. Sure, Willow had wanted to, but he should have had enough sense for both of them and talked her out of it. Talked to her about the dreams, about her counseling sessions—really any other reaction that *didn't* involve his penis.

Instead he fucked everything up.

He couldn't even try going back to just being friends with her—or some twisted version of friendship, at least—because he had cheated on his damn wife with her.

If he had *tried*, he couldn't have made a bigger mess of things.

Unsurprisingly, three days passed without a word from Willow. He wasn't sure that she even *wanted* to hear from him after that rather abrupt ending to what was essentially the night she lost her virginity....

On day four of no contact, he went out for groceries by himself and took the opportunity to send out a text message so he had some time to wait for her response. By the time he made it to the produce section, she had responded—just "hey back" but he hadn't expected much more than that.

"Free to talk?"

She sent back an affirmative, so he decided to go ahead and call her. Almost as soon as he pressed the last button, he realized he was still in public and close to home, so that was probably a mistake, but she answered before he could hang up.

"What are you doing?" she asked, in lieu of another greeting.

"Uh, shopping. Grocery shopping," he replied, grimacing at yet another reminder of his normal life. "What about you?"

"Facebook stalking you—your new baby is adorable."

An eyebrow shot up at her frank response. "I don't have a Facebook."

"Amanda does."

"Right." He couldn't really say much about that, seeing as he stalked her on a semi-regular basis. "Well…"

"Not that the other two aren't," she added. "They're all pretty adorable, but where did your daughter's brown hair come from? You and Amanda both have super black hair."

"This is not the conversation I expected to have," he stated.

Willow laughed. "Well, I haven't posted any new pictures on *my* profile. Wait, is it weird when I check you out, but not weird when you check me out?"

"No…it's plenty weird when I check you out," he replied, dryly. "You're the weird one for not being worried about that."

"Eh, if you wanted to murder me, you would have by now. Don't worry, I'm not trying to go all Fatal Attraction on your little family, I was just curious."

Since she so brashly introduced the topic, he decided to dive right in. "I'm sorry about the other night."

"It's fine," she assured him. "Not like I didn't know."

"Yeah… but knowing is one thing…. Anyway, I wanted to apologize if that made you uncomfortable. I thought I turned my phone off."

"Don't worry about it. I would've messaged you before, but… I wasn't sure."

He nodded, even though he knew she couldn't see him, but he couldn't seem to manufacture a response.

After several seconds of silence, she said, "Uh oh. Is that what this is?"

Was it? He hadn't really had a plan when he called, but if she was giving him the perfect opening…

Yet, when he opened his mouth, the words got stuck in his throat, and what ended up falling out instead was, "No. I just wanted to see… how you were doing. I felt bad."

"Oh. Well, good. I mean, not good that you felt bad— you don't have to feel bad."

• • •
*284*

"I kind of abandoned you," he pointed out. "And... right after..."

"It's not a big deal."

Frowning at her flippancy, he said, "Yes, it is. You deserved better than that."

Willow sighed, but didn't immediately respond. Finally, she said, "Ethan, I appreciate that, I do, but...I knew what I was getting into. You didn't invite me over and seduce me, remember? I'm the one who started it."

"You're... 18," he said on a sigh.

"I'm a mature 18," she said, her tone intentionally condescending. Then she laughed.

It made him strangely sad. "I don't know how long I can keep this up," he admitted.

Her laughter ebbed and the line fell silent.

"I don't...want to be that guy," he added. "I love my...family."

The silence stretched on as a woman reached across him to grab a crate of raspberries, her kid pestering her about ice cream. Ethan took a step back, glanced at his half empty cart, and then realized how ridiculous it was to be having this conversation in the middle of the produce section.

Abandoning his cart, he reached into his pocket and extracted his keys, heading for the privacy of his car.

He hit the parking lot before Willow drawled, "Okay. So, what does that mean?"

"I don't know," he said, his frustration with the whole situation evident in his voice. "I don't... I don't want to give you the wrong idea."

"I'm not fragile, Ethan. Just say what you mean."

It made him feel like such a prick, and he did wait until he slid into his driver's seat and shut the door before heaving a sigh and attempting a response. "I'm not...I don't want to lead you on. I like you—I *care* about you, and I want you to be happy."

"Ugh, if you're dumping me, don't be *that* guy, either, okay? Don't dump me for me. I can handle the truth."

"I'm not...*dumping* you, I just..." He sighed, leaning back against the headrest. "I'm not leaving my wife. I'm not... in a position to offer you *anything* more, and I don't ever intend to be." He paused, letting that sink in. "This isn't a temporary situation—if I could, if I didn't have a wife and kids, I would love to be with you. If I could split myself in two... like I have been, but now that line's been crossed, and I don't know how to..."

She gave him a few seconds to finish his thought, but when he didn't, she said, "Well, okay. So, what is it you want? Do you just want to go back to how it was before?"

"I don't know what that looks like now," he said honestly. "I didn't expect things to get this complicated."

"I didn't expect you to leave your wife, Ethan. I mean, I feel like you're making this more complicated than it needs to be. I enjoyed the other night, I won't lie, I wouldn't object to possibly revisiting, but if you can't, that's fine. I didn't expect to become your girlfriend or anything, I had mentally prepared myself for that, I just... I don't know, I thought we were friends."

"You have no more feelings for me than you have for any of your...male friends?"

"I didn't say that," she replied, a smile in her voice. "I just don't want you to be worried that I'm trying to start any drama in your life. I'm not. I have no agenda here, I'm no more interested than you are in hurting your pretty wife or tearing apart your family. I mean, let's be honest, you don't really fit into my life, either. It's not like I can bring you home to meet the parents. I'll make it simple—I'm down for whatever. I would prefer that we at least stay friends like we were before, but if you can't, I understand."

Closing his eyes, Ethan sighed. "You're insane, you know that."

"I prefer eccentric," she returned lightly. "I told you, I'm kind of a strange girl when it comes to relationships."

"I feel like I should have realized that already."

"Right? You're a terrible detective," she teased.

Ethan grinned helplessly. "Friends, then?"

"Friends," she agreed.

"Did it help?" he blurted.

"It gave me a nicer memory, so yes."

"You don't regret not making a nicer memory with someone else?"

Willow stifled a little chuckle. "It couldn't have been anyone else."

"Are you still going to make me jealous with your parade of boytoys?" he asked, smiling vaguely.

"Oh, without a doubt, friend. I mean, if you're going to keep stalking me."

"I probably will," he admitted. "It's a habit at this point."

"I don't mind. I'll be sure to post a few pictures you'll like. I've noticed you seem to like my legs."

He closed his eyes and shook his head. "Don't *torment* me, I'm only human."

She chuckled. "Well, if you're ever in the mood for Chinese food, you know my number."

"Temptress," he accused, but smiled anyway.

"Mm. Well, this feels too much like a break-up, and I don't like to linger with those, so I'm going to let you get back to your grocery shopping."

For some reason, he didn't want to hang up the phone. He didn't really have anything else to say either, but... he just didn't want to hang up.

Since he couldn't think of a good enough reason not to, he replied, "Okay."

Willow hesitated. "In case I don't hear from you for a while, try not to be too hard on yourself, okay? We both had some demons to deal with and...maybe we needed that separate life to work through it. If no one ever knows, what was the harm, right?"

"You and I know," he countered.

"It can be our little secret. I think telling her would have been a mistake—your family is obviously important to you, and I obviously don't know her at all, but... I think she's better off not knowing what happened."

"You mean about the other night...?"

"No," she said, simply. "Take care, Ethan."

It felt like goodbye—and he liked it even less than he expected to. He watched the numbers blink, letting him know that their conversation hadn't even lasted six whole minutes.

He had expected to feel better after having "the talk" with Willow, not...bereft. Sure, she had left a sort of open invitation, but it felt like they both knew he couldn't take her up on it. If he did, he would feel even worse.

What a shitty hole he found himself in.

After a moment, he collected his thoughts and headed back into the grocery store. Before he grabbed a new cart, he figured he would go back to the produce section to see if the other one was gone.

It wasn't.

There, parked crookedly next to the display of raspberries and blueberries, his cart waited for him as if he had never been gone, each item just as he had left it.

Of course, it hadn't even been six minutes.

It felt like much longer than that.

---

Pulling into his driveway, Ethan turned off the car and turned to the passenger seat, quickly searching for the bag with the eggs. Locating them, he placed the eggs on the dash board while he loaded his arms up with bags, satisfied that he would only have to make one trip. He managed to grab the bag of eggs last, but then he realized he wasn't going to be able to unlock the door, so he hoped Amanda hadn't locked it behind him.

By the time he made it to the door, his fingers were freezing from the wind chill and he didn't want to crouch and risk dropping the groceries, so instead, he lightly kicked the door a few times, hoping it would catch Amanda's attention.

A moment passed—nothing.

Sighing heavily, he crouched down, shifting the bags of groceries in his arms and managing to turn the knob until, thankfully, the door cracked open.

The house was quiet, so he figured the baby must be sleeping, but he was surprised Alison didn't immediately come rushing in to greet him. Maybe she was upstairs.

He was just about to turn toward the kitchen when he heard a muffled sound from the living room.

Turning toward the noise, Ethan was startled to see not his wife, but a heavy man in a black jacket and jeans.

His first thought was his gun—he didn't have his gun, but then he looked beyond that man—and the four other dubious looking men—and saw Amanda, tied to a chair with duct tape over her mouth, and beside her, in another wooden chair, also bound with rope and duct tape, Alison.

# CHAPTER TWENTY TWO

All of the bags hit the ground at once.

The color drained out of Ethan's face.

On the couch, watching Ethan with a vague expression of boredom, was an older man with salt and pepper hair, nearly as dark as Ethan's at one time. His nose was long and sloped over a mouth that seemed to be set in a permanent snarl. Bushy eyebrows furrowed above his steely gray eyes as he met Ethan's gaze.

Antonio Castellanos.

Willow's father.

Adrenaline surged through Ethan's body—useless fucking adrenaline.

His stomach pitched and the bones in his legs seemed to melt, but he somehow managed to carry himself mechanically into the living room, his gaze jumping away from the other man's, back to his wife, his daughter.

Where were his sons?

He couldn't breathe.

He tried to open his mouth, but it was like he was having a stroke—his body wouldn't listen to his brain.

"Ethan Wilde," the older man said idly, the menace in his tone quite deliberate. "Do you know who I am?"

His tongue was trapped in his mouth and Ethan could only manage a nod.

The other man's bushy eyebrows shot up. "Good, good. Did you know who I was before you raped my daughter?"

A noise escaped Amanda, sort of a gasp tinged with horror that made Ethan flinch. He couldn't look at her—didn't know how to respond.

Legs finally giving out, Ethan fell to his knees. The older man watched, his expression unreadable.

Ethan knew he was as good as dead.

His incredible luck had run out.

"Please... leave my family out of this," he managed, meeting Antonio's gaze.

"You didn't answer my question."

A lump rose in his throat, shame washing over him at the thought of having to admit to such a heinous act with his wife and daughter watching.

"Where are my sons?"

Antonio glanced at a spot above and behind Ethan, but before he had a chance to wonder what the man was looking at, he heard almost a whistling sound—and then burning pain on his right side that literally knocked him over.

He grabbed his right arm as he heard Amanda and Alison cry out behind him, and it took him a moment to connect the pain on his right side to the thug holding a baseball bat, staring down at him.

"Let's try that again," Antonio said. "Did you know—?"

"Yes," Ethan said, briefly closing his eyes, wishing he was just having a really fucking terrible dream.

"Yes, you knew that Willow was my daughter?"

He stomach roiled and it took real effort not to vomit all over the carpet. "Yes, I knew that she was your daughter."

"Huh," the older man murmured. "That's a brave thing to admit."

"Can we please... I have a study, can we please discuss this in my study, away from my family? They have nothing to do with this. Please."

"Why? Your wife doesn't know?" The older man feigned surprise.

"My daughter is eight years old," Ethan stated.

"Mine's 18," Antonio responded, his tone hard and cold.

"Please."

"You're not budgeting your time very wisely, Ethan," the older man informed him. "If I were in your place right now, I'm pretty sure location is the last thing I would be worried about."

The old man pulled out a cell phone and began fidgeting with it. Ethan took advantage of the momentary distraction to steal a glimpse of Amanda—and then he wished he hadn't. He couldn't even hold her gaze as she stared at him, her blue eyes round with horror. Beside her, Alison was so terrified she was bawling.

*What have I done?*

"I'm so sorry," he whispered, barely able to find his voice.

Antonio flicked a glance in Ethan's direction, but saw that he was staring at Amanda.

Then there was noise—static, like a microphone brushing against fabric, and then he heard a voice that he recognized—then another.

On the cell phone, which Antonio held facing them, was a video.

Willow was on her knees in that dingy, piece of shit hellhole, her back to the camera, but Ethan was facing the camera, his eyes closed as her head moved back and forth in front of his crotch.

The blood in his veins turned to ice.

It must have been the tail end, because then Willow was getting to her feet and Ethan wanted to die as he listened to himself say he needed a condom.

"Turn it off," he said, covering his mouth as bile rose up in his throat. Tears burned behind his eyes and he jerked in Alison's direction, but she was still crying and hadn't seemed to notice the phone.

"Imagine how *I* felt the first time I saw this."

Still fighting back nausea, Ethan pushed himself up off the ground and forced himself to stand, even as the man with the baseball bat shifted his weight, caressing the wood deliberately.

On the video, Ethan was already pumping into Willow for all the living room to see, but the bastard finally pushed a button on the top of the phone and the screen went black, the sound cutting off.

"I didn't want to hurt her. I didn't have a choice."

"We always have choices, Ethan," Antonio stated, abruptly coming to his feet.

"They would have killed me if they knew—I was there to save her, I never wanted to hurt her. I tried to talk them out of it, I tried to convince them to just—just ransom her if they needed—"

"You chose your life over my daughter's," Antonio stated, raising his voice. "Makes sense, anyone would have done the same. Too bad for you, Willow isn't just anyone, and as it happens, her life is worth much more than yours."

"Please, Mr. Castellanos, I swear to God, I didn't want to hurt your daughter. For what it's worth, I protected her afterward. I didn't let anyone else hurt her and I made sure she was returned home safely—"

The man cut him off. "Now, the most appropriate payback, obviously, would be to steal your daughter's innocence like you stole mine."

Ethan's whole body went rigid, his blood running cold.

Antonio's lips tilted up just slightly. "However, I don't make a habit of keeping pedophiles on my payroll. So tell me how this sounds. Instead of your daughter, one of the guys here will rape your wife—I'd do it myself, but I prefer blondes. While that's going on, you can have a front row seat while they ransack your house to make it look like a break in, and then put a bullet in each one of their pretty little heads. But don't worry, you won't be suffering long—I have a third bullet with your name on it."

Behind him, Amanda moaned—a gut-wrenching sound of grief, emanating from her and attacking him more effectively than a physical blow.

As his world crumbled around him, Ethan said the only thing he could possibly think to say.

"Your daughter's in love with me."

That wiped the smirk right off of Antonio's face, and gave Ethan a shred of hope.

"Excuse me?" Antonio replied, bushy brows shooting halfway up his forehead.

"Call Willow—please, she wouldn't want this. She'll never forgive you if you do this. I understand why you feel this way, I would, too, but I'm telling you, if you do this, Willow will never have anything to do with you again. She may not be returning your phone calls right now, but she still cares, she still…loves you, but if you do this, if you hurt my family, if you kill me—she'll never forgive you for that."

For a moment, he said nothing, then very slowly, he ground out, "Am I to understand that your reasoning…for me not to kill you… is that you have been *fucking* my daughter— that you *raped* when she was helpless and in captivity?"

Ethan swallowed, second guessing the logic of such a move, but all out of other moves. It wasn't like his world could implode *more*.

"Call her. Or I can," he pleaded. "I wasn't—I only wanted to help her, I wanted her to know that I was sorry for what happened, but she needed someone to talk to, and…she didn't feel like anyone who wasn't there with her could understand. She's—she's completely forgiven me, this vengeance—it's wasted on her at this point. She doesn't hate me anymore, she understands the position I was in and she knows how sorry I am for hurting her. As much as she's already lost, would you really want to take something else from her? Please…call her, she'll tell you exactly what I'm telling you."

At least he fucking hoped she would.

"If I call my daughter right now, she'll tell me how in love with you she is and how she'll hate me forever if I take out her rapist?" the older man asked skeptically.

That sounded much less likely, but since he had already made the claim, Ethan could only nod, his stomach twisting up in knots.

Antonio nodded his head at one of the men standing behind Ethan, and the man approached the chair Alison was tied to. Ethan didn't immediately understand what was happening until he saw the gun moving toward his daughter's head, heard Amanda's muffled wailing. His whole body tensed and then, without regard for anything else, he prepared to lunge at the man, as useless as that would be in the long run.

"Ethan," Antonio snapped.

The blood was rushing everywhere, surging in his brain, his ears, he could barely concentrate, even as he realized the man with the gun had stopped moving and the gun wasn't aimed at Alison.

The threat was there though.

He stood guard by her chair, gun in one hand, the other hand resting on the back of the chair.

Alison's face was so red, her eyes crinkled up as she cried.

Ethan wanted to die.

Tears of helplessness and regret burned behind his eyes and he didn't even want to defend himself anymore. He deserved Antonio's wrath, he deserved a fucking bullet between his eyes—but his family didn't.

Sinking back to his knees, a million different thoughts flashed through his mind—the first time he had ever held Alison in his arms, her little face all red, her tiny hand wrapped around his finger while she slept. Her first day of kindergarten, going into the building nervous, and coming home with a big grin on her face. When she met her little brother for the first time and she was so excited—then in mere days, a little jealous. Amanda, so miserably pregnant with Caleb, but forcing herself to walk through the whole zoo because it was what Alison wanted to do for her birthday. Jackson stealing Alison's Christmas presents from under the tree when he was barely crawling. Amanda cuddling with him on the couch before they were married, wearing his favorite black dress with her hair all around his face. Seeing Willow for the first time, trussed up and terrified...and then in front of him, with his hands on her.

Bringing his gaze back to Antonio, he saw the man's lip curl up as the video briefly began playing again before he quickly cleared it from the screen and brought up the keypad.

"You better hope you're right about my daughter's affection for you."

Ethan suddenly wished he wouldn't have made that call at the grocery store—the one she took as a break-up.

It hit him right in the gut that he could be making a mistake—even if Willow wasn't a vengeful person, she had certainly never claimed to love him, and if Antonio didn't give her any details, she wasn't likely to make such a claim. How would she know to?

"Could I call her?" Ethan asked.

Antonio merely shook his head as he placed the phone to his ear and waited.

It felt like the phone was ringing for an eternity. The room wasn't quiet enough to hear through the phone, but eventually the older man ended the call without ever speaking.

She hadn't answered the goddamn phone.

Antonio's eyebrows shot up. "Too bad."

"Let me call her. I just talked to her maybe a half hour ago. She'll answer if I call."

He was making a lot of promises he couldn't keep, but he couldn't seem to stop.

For a moment, the older man merely stared at Ethan, then he finally nodded his head. "Reach for the phone slowly—don't try anything stupid."

"I won't," Ethan promised, fumbling for the phone in his pocket. His hands shook as he unlocked the screen, his fingers unsteadily tapping in his passcode, and then he dialed her number, praying that she would pick up the phone.

"Put it on speaker," Antonio commanded.

Ethan pressed the speaker button and waited one ring, then two.

"Hey," she answered, her tone warm.

For the first time since he walked in the door, he felt like he could actually breathe.

"Willow," he said, although it sounded almost like a groan to his own ears. "Thank God you answered the phone."

She laughed. "Miss me already, friend?"

"Willow, your dad is in my living room—"

"No specifics," Antonio barked, his eyes burning irritably.

"What?" she demanded, clearly confused. "What are you talking about? Am I on speaker?"

"Hi, honey," Antonio called.

"Dad?" she asked, disbelievingly. "Oh my God, what are you doing?"

"I need you to answer a question for me," Antonio called loudly, as if she couldn't hear him through the cell phone.

"Is someone crying?" she demanded.

Alison was still crying, and one glance toward the girls was incapacitating—Amanda's face was red, tears streaming down her cheeks, and she was looking at him with a kind of loathing he had never seen on anybody's face before.

Not that he could blame her.

Even if he made it out alive, what was going to be left of his life?

"I was just paying your buddy a little visit—"

"Who's crying?" she interrupted, her voice wavering as it rose. "What have you done?"

"Nothing. Calm down," Antonio replied, his tone that of a man clearly used to being in charge.

Willow took an audible breath. "Ethan?"

"I'm here," he replied tensely. "Willow, I need you to—"

Antonio cut him off. "Your *friend* here, he the same guy that raped you?"

The only immediate response was dead silence.

After a moment, he replied, "That sounds like a yes."

"It—how did you—? It's not that simple—I don't know who told you what, but he didn't... he didn't...."

"I saw a video," Antonio stated.

"What?" she whispered raggedly.

Antonio's lips pressed together, the fury on his face growing as he looked at Ethan.

"He didn't—I don't want to talk about that. You need to leave, right now, Dad."

"Is this the guy or not?" Antonio pressed.

She hesitated. "Yes, technically, but it's complicated and I'm not angry at him anymore and I do *not* want you to be at his house, do you understand me? Leave him alone."

"Do you love this asshole?"

Her breath caught. Instead of answering, she took on a warning tone. "Dad, please leave him *alone*."

Antonio shrugged at Ethan, as if mildly disappointed. "All right, baby. I'll talk to you later, okay?"

The man did not look appeased, not at all, and although Willow was telling her father to leave him alone, Ethan was increasingly aware that she had not backed up his presumptuous claims—not at all.

"Willow," he said, his voice rising a bit.

"Do you hear me, Dad?" she demanded, her voice rising in response to his. "Dad?"

"Yeah, I heard you. I have some things to take care of."

"Yes," she blurted. "Yes, to all of it, goddammit. You don't know the whole story, you don't know what's been going on—you never even called to *check* on me, so I definitely don't need you out seeking vengeance on my behalf. If you hurt Ethan, I swear to God, I'll turn this conversation over to the police."

Eyebrows quirking, Antonio said, "Huh. Already he's more important to you than family, huh?"

"Ethan *is* my family," she stated, so immediately and so immovably that it gave even Ethan pause.

"I see," the other man said lowly. Then, eyebrows knitting together, he said, "Did he knock you up?"

She sighed. "No, I don't mean… no, but I do love him and if anything happens to him…"

Whether it was a threat or a statement, he didn't know, because she didn't finish the thought.

"I see," Antonio said again.

Ethan waited with bated breath to see how the older man would respond that time, but he seemed to be taking his time mulling it over.

"I'm serious, Dad. Leave him alone, okay? Please?"

"All right." Nodding at Ethan, he said, "You can hang up now."

"Should I come over?" Willow asked uncertainly.

"No," Antonio answered, before Ethan could. "You stay home, we're going to clear out of here. Does your mom know about this?"

"N-no. And I would like to keep it that way. Not a hair on his head, Dad."

"I got it, Willow." He looked at Ethan a little more harshly.

"Thanks," Ethan murmured, before ending the call.

Thanks seemed a little insufficient, but what else could he say?

Lifting one bushy eyebrow, the older man said, "She just saved your ass."

"Not for the first time," Ethan muttered.

Relief washed over him as the man next to Alison's chair began untying her while another untied Amanda. Antonio moved so that he was standing in front of Amanda, his figure imposing as he ripped the tape off her mouth.

"I expect that all of you are smart enough not to say anything about this little meeting?"

Amanda nodded vigorously, scrubbing her wet cheeks with the heels of her hands.

Once freed from the restraints, Alison flung herself at him, crying, "Daddy!"

Ethan squeezed her as tightly as he could without hurting her, closing his eyes as she buried her face in the crook of his neck. "I'm so sorry, baby. I'm so sorry."

He just kept murmuring it, over and over, as he rocked back and forth with her.

Ethan expected Antonio to have something more to say to him, perhaps along the lines of, "If you hurt my daughter, I'm going to empty a clip into your face" but instead, the man simply rounded up his minions and left as suddenly as he had appeared.

Before they even made it to their cars, which he now realized were parked on the street (something he should have noticed, but he'd been too busy thinking about the phone call to Willow), Amanda was flying past him and up the stairs.

He tried to reassure Alison, to convince her it had only been a game that they would never play again, but he couldn't get past the fear he had felt moments earlier himself, so he wasn't sure how he could expect her to.

When she finally calmed down a little, he asked if they could go upstairs to check on Mommy.

Upon entering their bedroom, he was hit with relief at the sight of his two sons, safe and seemingly unaware that there had been any danger.

Amanda had a suitcase thrown open and was shoving clothing into every crevice.

"Amanda…"

"Don't," she said, shaking her head, not looking at him.

Alison was holding onto his hand, but he loosened her grip and bent down. "Can you take your brothers into the other room to play for a few minutes?"

Ever the dutiful sister, she nodded her head and wrangled Jackson into the other room. Ethan picked up Caleb and took him in, placing him on his play mat and closing the door behind him so no one escaped.

With no small amount of dread, he went back to the bedroom to face Amanda.

"I honestly don't want to talk to you right now," she stated.

"I know that what you heard down there…was—"

"Was it true?" she interrupted, still not looking at him.

He paused for a few seconds. "It's complicated."

"It's not complicated," she said, looking up at him sharply before looking away again. "It's the easiest fucking thing in the world—did you rape a girl? Most people can pretty easily answer this question without having to think about it."

Ethan sighed, brushing a hand through his hair. "I didn't have a choice, Amanda—not really. If they realized I wasn't who they thought I was, I would have put *all* of us in danger. I might never have come home. They could've killed me. It's not like I did it because I *wanted* to."

"Didn't you, on some level?" she shot back.

"That's fucked up, Amanda."

"You're right, it is fucked up, Ethan, but you're fucking her now, aren't you?"

He averted his gaze, and Amanda nodded.

"You're unbelievable. I honestly don't even know who you are anymore."

"I'm so sorry."

Something between a sob and a laugh shot out of her. "That is *so far* from being a good enough response, Ethan."

"I didn't mean for any of this to happen."

"Please, feed me another generic line." She punctuated the sentence by ripping her cell phone charger out of the wall and throwing it in her suit case.

"Please don't leave," he said quietly.

"I don't see that I have a choice. If you think I'm sleeping in this bed next to you tonight, you're more delusional than you sound right now."

He couldn't really argue that. "Okay. Look, if someone has to leave, I'll leave. Stop packing, I'll—"

That time she looked up at him, her expression wounded. "No, Ethan, *we're* leaving. I don't feel safe in my own fucking house right now—and who the hell was that man? I have so many…fucking questions that I don't even want to know the answers to. How could you keep all of this from me?"

Guilt walloped him. "It wasn't easy. I… didn't want you to… I thought I could shoulder it on my own and you'd never have to know."

Her eyebrows shot up. "Never have to know that the father of my children is a rapist? How magnanimous of you."

His jaw locked—it was difficult not to be defensive with words like that being thrown at him. "Would you have preferred that I died? Because I would have. The ringleader didn't fully trust me even *after* I did it, and since he was going to have me killed when I blew my cover, I'm pretty goddamn sure that I would have died before I ever got to tell the cops where the girls were being taken, so not only would I be dead right now, but all three of the girls who are home with their families right now—hurt, yes, but alive, and not living in forced prostitution—*would* be living in forced prostitution in the very best of scenarios. I'm not saying it's okay, but I *literally* had no better option."

Amanda hung her head, rifling through the suitcase. "And that may be true, Ethan, but it doesn't mean I can forgive you. It isn't my *place* to forgive you, honestly."

"Give it time," he said gently. "Even she forgave me."

At that, her mouth thinned into a hard little line. "Yeah, I heard."

"I'm so sorry, Amanda. It isn't what you're thinking— what it sounded like downstairs."

"So you're not fucking her, then?" she asked, looking up at him sharply, daring him to lie to her.

He forced himself to hold her gaze. "It was only once. I know that doesn't make it better, but…" He had to avert his gaze then, sighing. "She was a goddamn virgin, Amanda. Lane and his band of psychopaths cheated her out of her first time, and…I was trying to help her."

"With your dick," she supplied.

"No, it wasn't like that. We… were just sort of survivors of the same horrible experience at first, she couldn't assimilate back into her life, she was haunted by dreams, she was afraid…to even walk out on her front porch after the sun went down. I felt terrible, and I just wanted to make it right. I just… I can't even explain it, Amanda, because it sounds so much more fucked up than it was. She needed a friend."

Amanda shook her head wordlessly. After a minute passed, she said, "I need you to get Alison's suitcase out of the closet, I can't reach it."

After Amanda disappeared into the bathroom, Ethan closed his eyes for a few seconds, then he slowly made his way to the closet to get his daughter's suitcase.

# CHAPTER TWENTY THREE

"Why isn't Daddy coming?"

Ethan stood by the driver's side window, forcing down the instinct to beg Amanda to reconsider—not in front of the kids.

"I told you, we're going to go to the American Girl store and get you a new doll, then we're going to get ice cream and have a little hotel party, just us."

"But Daddy likes ice cream," Alison stated.

"Daddy has to work," Amanda stated.

Pouting, she crossed her arms and slunk back in her seat. "That's not fair."

"What about me?" Jackson demanded. "I don't want a doll."

"We'll get you a toy, too, don't worry about it," Amanda said. Glancing in Ethan's direction, she held his gaze only for a second before looking away again.

"I'll talk to you tomorrow?" he asked.

She nodded her head, but not with much conviction. Since he couldn't argue with the kids listening, he took a step back and redirected his gaze to the backseat with a manufactured smile as he waved goodbye to his kids.

Once the car was out of view, he was consumed by emptiness.

It had been a longshot, but he had hoped that somehow he could convince Amanda not to go, find the words to explain things to her in a way that she would understand, even if she was still furious at him.

Even worse, when he had helped carry the suitcases out to the car, she hadn't seemed furious, just tired. Defeated. As if she had already lost a battle that he wasn't even aware they'd had—or that she'd won, but it didn't feel much like winning.

It was impossible not to worry that once she left, she wouldn't come back.

How could he expect her to come to terms with what had happened when he had barely even done that himself—and he'd had five months?

Such a short time ago, his life had been intact.

Now everything was a mess. Not only had he wrecked everything they'd built together, but he didn't know how to fix it.

What if he couldn't? How would she ever be able to trust him again? What did she see now when she looked at him?

If he just gave her some time, maybe everything would be okay.

It felt like a lie even as the thought went through his head, but he had nothing else to hold onto, so he had to try to believe it.

Since he was still rooted to the spot he had been standing in when he watched his family disappear, he knew as soon as he saw headlights turning into his driveway that it was Willow.

Practically before she even turned the car off, she threw open the door and jumped out.

The mere sight of her filled him with a relief he didn't completely understand. A moment earlier, he wouldn't have said that he wanted to see her, but now that she was there, she felt like exactly what he needed.

Wordlessly, she approached him and threw her arms around him. One arm tightened around her waist while the other tangled in her hair, holding her against his chest.

"Are you okay?" she finally asked, quietly.

"Yeah," he murmured.

Willow hesitated. "I drove by the first time. I saw suitcases…"

He nodded slightly. "Amanda left."

Tucking her head down into his chest and squeezing him, she said, "I'm *so* sorry."

"Not your fault."

"I mean, it kind of is," she replied. "I didn't know what to say, I just didn't want him to hurt you. I figured you could explain after the fact…"

"I tried, but it's not… I mean, you know how fucked up it is, how do I explain that?"

For several seconds, she was quiet, then she said, "If you think it would help, I could… talk to her. Not even to explain it, I could just say I was lying about everything to my dad to save you because I understood the circumstances."

He shook his head. "I told her the truth, no point trying to lie about it now."

"Oh. Well… I'm sorry."

Instead of answering, he lightly ran his hand up the back of her shirt, noting that her skin was cool, and she was only wearing a thin sweater with no coat.

"You're cold," he finally said. "We shouldn't keep standing out here."

Casting an apprehensive glance at his house, she lifted her eyebrows.

Understanding her wordless hesitation, he nodded. "I don't really want to be here right now either."

"Maybe we could get a room?" she suggested, somewhat hesitantly.

Glancing down at her, he said, "I'm not sure what's going on with my family, Willow... I mean, I'm still hoping they come back..."

"I know," she said quickly, holding his gaze. "I figured you might need a friend."

The corners of his lips tilted upward. "Yeah, I could probably use one of those."

Willow flashed him a little smile. "Well, you're in luck. Unless you want to be alone?"

Ethan shook his head. "No, I don't want to be alone."

Skimming her fingers along his sides, she replied, "Good."

---

They barely made it inside the hotel room before Ethan dropped his bag, turning Willow to face him and backing her against the wall. Her warm gaze met his and she smiled softly, gripping his hips and pulling him up against her.

"Did you ask for this room, or should I reevaluate my opinion of Fate?"

Ethan chuckled. "I requested it."

"You're such a romantic," she teased, rolling her eyes.

"Oh yeah, that's me, Mr. Romantic," he said dryly, leaning in to trail kisses up her neck.

Tilting her neck to give him better access, she said, "Deny it all you want, actions speak louder than words."

"I just wanted the room with the Jacuzzi," he murmured, his fingers brushing against her stomach, fingering the button on her jeans.

"Oh yeah? Why's that?"

"I've imagined doing unspeakably pleasurable things to you in that Jacuzzi."

"Ooh, unspeakably pleasurable? We might have to make that a reality."

Reaching for the hem of her sweater, he grabbed it and pulled it over her head, tossing it on the floor. His mouth went back to her neck, starting at the top and making his way down to her collar bone, then lower, leaving lingering kisses along her breasts as his hand made its way down her hip, over the curve of her ass and squeezing.

Releasing a little moan as she squirmed against him, Willow asked, "Should we move this to the bed?"

Smiling slightly, he brushed a lock of hair behind her ear and took her hand, leading her over to the bed.

---

"I should probably go home soon."

Willow was curled up in Ethan's arms, her hair damp

"Yeah, your family is probably getting worried."

"I don't want to go," she said.

Smiling a little, he said, "I wish you could stay."

"I was so afraid when you called me earlier."

"Yeah, so was I. Thanks for saving my ass, by the way."

"Anytime," she said dryly.

"This is, what, the second or third time?"

"Who's keeping track." She placed a little kiss on his chest, right over his heart. "I realized today that I would be pretty pissed if you died."

"I can't say I'd be very happy about it, either," he agreed, rubbing his hand up and down her arm.

For a moment, they were quiet, just lying there together, tangled up in the sheets. Tenderness swept over him and he shifted, lightly tilting her face to look up at him. She smiled softly, her gray eyes brimming with affection, but still with dark smudges beneath them.

A slight crease marred his brow. "Can I ask you a serious question?"

"Of course."

"How are you sleeping?"

Her own smile weakened, but she didn't get as defensive as she had. Her voice held no hostility, only patience when she said, "I told you I didn't want to talk about that. It's not a big deal."

"It *is* a big deal," he disagreed. "It isn't healthy. Have you told your counselor? Maybe some sleeping pills would help."

Willow shook her head mutely, her fingers drawing little circles over his stomach.

"I hate being the person responsible for your bad memories."

She glanced back up at him, then drew her hand up to caress his face, smiling faintly. "You're not—not all of them."

"Even one would be too many."

"You're responsible for plenty of good ones, too," she informed him.

"Oh yeah?" He quirked an eyebrow, almost smiling. "Like what?"

Her voice turned teasing and her smile more whimsical as she drawled, "Like…you being jealous of a scrawny teenager."

She finished on a laugh, so he gathered her into a hug and squeezed her sides, smiling in denial. "No."

"Yes," she said, a little smugly, grinning at him. "And getting Chinese food."

"We do like Chinese food."

"This hotel room—twice now," she added, lifting an eyebrow suggestively. "That night by the basketball court."

"That wasn't a good memory," he reminded her.

"Part of it was. For me, anyway. I hadn't admitted before then that I liked you."

"Okay, I get the point. Good memories with the bad."

Willow nodded. "I like tonight—just this chunk of it. Might be top three material."

"Top three, huh? What are the other two?"

"I'll never tell." She winked.

Ethan smirked, tugging her closer, lingering with his mouth hovering over hers. "I bet I can get it out of you."

Running her fingers through his hair and dipping an inch closer, she said, "Maybe if you try really hard."

His lips met hers again, and it was just as electric as always. Willow moved, straddling him as his hands skated up her back, arching at her sensitivity to his touch. It was so easy to get completely wrapped up in him, completely disconnected from time and space—it was just him and her, and nothing else.

She could swear the bed was actually vibrating.

Ethan broke away, frowning slightly. "What is that?"

"Hm?" she asked, a bit incoherently.

He twisted and looked past her toward the foot of the bed, where his pants were hanging halfway off the mattress.

And they *were* vibrating.

"Oh, shit," he said. Willow climbed off of him and turned to sit with her legs crossed while he fished around in his pants, trying to find his phone.

He looked at the screen for a split second, then answered with a gruff, "Hello?"

"Hey, it's me. Are you at home?"

"Uh, not right this second. Why?"

"I forgot Jackson's giraffe at the house, he refuses to sleep without it. Could you possibly bring it out here?"

"Yeah, of course."

"All right." There was a brief, awkward pause. "I'll send you the address."

"Okay, I'll be there in…a little less than an hour, probably."

"Fine." Another awkward pause. "Bye."

Shoulders slumping, Ethan ended the call and turned back to Willow, grimacing apologetically.

Offering a thin smile, she climbed off the bed, bending to pick up her clothes.

"I'm sorry," he said.

"No problem, I was about to leave anyway."

"My…son forgot his giraffe—he's been sleeping with it since he was a baby, and he won't go to sleep without it."

"It's fine, really," she assured him, tossing him another smile as she tugged on her jeans. Once her bra was on, she approached him, leaning up against him and giving him a brief kiss. "You're a good dad. It's sweet."

"Speaking of dads, do you think yours is keeping eyes on me right now?"

Willow rolled her eyes. "Ugh. I have no idea. I'm going to call him tomorrow and talk to him. I'll call you after to let you know how it goes."

"Sounds good."

# CHAPTER TWENTY FOUR

When Willow arrived home, she was still thinking about
Ethan.

There was a chill in the air and she was still without a
coat, so she hurried up the front porch steps.

It seemed the height of insanity to think of it as a *good*
day—it certainly hadn't started out that way. As the day wore
on, it only seemed to get progressively worse.

Until she was in Ethan's arms. Then, as usual,
everything felt better—her troubles far away, her heart
foolishly brimming, and even if only for a few hours, she had
peace.

Although, with the implosion of his family, perhaps it
would end up being more than a few hours.

Just thinking about what her father had done made her
stomach twist up in knots. She *definitely* needed to have a talk
with him, to make sure he understood Ethan and his family
were completely off-limits. How to successfully convey that,
she wasn't completely sure, but she would figure it out.

God, that was going to be an awkward conversation.

When she closed the door behind her, rubbing her arms in hopes the friction and the heat from the house would join teams and instantly warm her bones, she thought she heard a gasp.

Jerking her head toward the sound, she saw both of her moms heading straight for her, Lauren with her hands covering her mouth, Ashlynn looking years older than she had when she left the house earlier.

Already weary, Willow offered up a quick apology. "I'm sorry, I didn't mean to worry you; my phone died. I'm fine."

"Did you go to him?" Lauren's brown eyes flared angrily, then immediately turned sad again.

"What?" Willow asked, bewildered.

Ashlynn's mouth curved down, then she pressed her lips together and stood a little taller. "Your father stopped by."

Just like that, the world stopped moving. Time stood still. Her blood paused on its way through her veins and her heart ceased to beat.

Then a burst of hot fury coursed through her, jumpstarting her heart and triggering a weird popping sound in the vicinity of her brain.

The sorrow oozing out of Ashlynn's expression only served to infuriate her more.

"He had no right," Willow finally bit out.

"You weren't going to tell us," Lauren cried, her heightened emotionality aggravating Willow even more. "We needed to know!"

"No, you didn't! Because it had nothing to do with you—it was *my* experience, *my* choice whether or not to tell you or anyone else."

"Honey—you need help."

Ashlynn put a hand on Lauren's shoulder, obviously aware that was not the right thing to say. "What your mother means to say—"

Putting a hand up to signal stop, she said, "I don't care. I don't care what she means to say. I'm not going to talk about this, because *I* didn't choose to talk about this. You don't know the story and my father is a fucking psychopath, so I'm not sure why you would listen to him anyway."

"Willow," Ashlynn called after her, but Willow stormed upstairs.

By the time she got to her room, she could feel angry tears at the corners of her eyes, and all she wanted to do was escape.

With that thought in mind, she went to her closet and ripped her small suitcase out, throwing it on her bed and then going to her dresser drawer. Her mind was racing, reminding her of her relative helplessness; where did she think she was going to go? All of her female friends were distant memories and she didn't want to go to a male friend.

Ethan. The simplest answer, staring right at her. He had rented a hotel for the night, surely she could stay with him while she cooled off.

Before she could grab her phone out of her purse to text him, her parents were already invading her bedroom, effectively blocking the exit with their collaborative suffering.

"I'm sorry we found out this way," Ashlynn began. "I truly am, honey—we didn't go searching for this information, we didn't violate your privacy to find out."

"Whatever."

Lauren watched her daughter throw clothing into the suitcase and burst out, "What are you *doing*? You need to talk to us."

"That's hilarious coming from you," Willow stated. "Just go to sleep, you won't even remember anything bad happened in the morning."

Lauren flinched. That pissed Ashlynn off.

"Now listen here," she began firmly. "We are sorry that you are hurting, but you would do well to remember who is responsible for that pain, because it sure as hell isn't us."

Somehow hearing that made the burning behind her eyes return, further pissing her off. Since she had nothing nice to say, she said nothing at all.

"You're not leaving this house, Willow," Ashlynn stated.

"I'm not staying here," she stated, shaking her head.

"You're not going to him," Lauren blurted angrily, her voice rising. "My god, how could you—"

Ashlynn interrupted. "We're just worried about you."

"I'm *fine*."

"Clearly you aren't, honey. And that's perfectly understandable—what happened to you—"

"Stop." Just the lead-in was making her feel queasy. "I've dealt with everything that happened, I don't want to talk about it with you, not now and maybe not ever. I just want you to forget whatever that asshole said to you. I'm sure most of it wasn't even true."

"You weren't raped?" Lauren asked sharply, coming more unhinged by the second. Her eye twitched before she went on. "That piece of shit didn't rape you at gunpoint?"

Her stomach pitched, mental images popping up and warring with the fierce protectiveness she felt over Ethan.

"You didn't start—" Lauren's voice broke halfway through as she tried to fight back a sob. "You didn't start *sleeping with* him afterward? You didn't sleep with your married rapist—?"

"Okay, Lauren, calm down," Ashlynn said, squeezing Lauren's shoulder. "You're coming off as very judgey right now."

Lauren's eyes bulged. "Do you hear the words that are coming out of my mouth?"

"It is not her fault. He's a grown man, for god's sake. He took advantage of her when she was at her most vulnerable."

"Oh my god, I'm standing right here," Willow objected. "Ethan did not take advantage of me, not at all. You have no idea what you're talking about."

"You can't be in a relationship with your rapist, Willow!"

"You don't—he is not my *rapist*. You don't even know the situation—"

"I don't *need* to know the situation! I have all the information I need. Did he rape you? If yes, then no relationship! Easy."

Clenching her fists in frustration, Willow could only shake her head. She understood their reactions, but they weren't seeing it through her eyes—nor could they. "You don't get it. It doesn't matter. It isn't your decision to make."

"I don't even know what to say to you right now," Lauren stated, shaking her head in disbelief. "What would possess you—?"

Ashlynn took a step toward Willow. "Honey, none of this is your fault, but you aren't seeing things clearly. Did he protect you before it happened? Or...after?"

Giving Ashlynn her most withering glare, she said, "It has *nothing* to do with that, but yes, as a matter of fact; if not for him, probably every guy in the fucking house would have had a turn."

It was a cruel mental image to fling at them, and while Lauren made a pitiful little noise, even the more formidable Ashlynn grimaced.

Between sobs, Lauren said, "That's no excuse. You can't be the kind of girl who—"

Spinning around, Ashlynn said, "Please let me talk to her alone for a few minutes. Please. You're too emotional, you need to...you need to take a moment and collect yourself before you say something you can never take back."

"This is our fault," Lauren cried, ignoring Ashlynn. "We never should've had him over for that dinner. We invited a predator into our home."

"This is no one's *fault*. He is not a predator. This has all been blown way out of proportion," Willow insisted, grabbing her purse and digging around for her phone.

Ashlynn's eyes followed the movement. "What are you doing?"

"I'm getting my phone," Willow stated as she pulled it out of her bag.

"Who are you calling?" Lauren asked, taking a few steps closer, peering at the phone.

"I'm going to stay with a friend for the night. You guys...I can't handle this right now."

As her thumb moved toward the green icon that would eventually connect her to Ethan, Willow saw a shadow approaching, but didn't connect the dots until Lauren snatched the phone right out of her hand, her eyes wide, the pupils dilated.

"Hey!" Willow objected, grabbing for it.

Lauren jerked it back, still bug-eyed. "You seriously think I'm going to let you call him? Have you lost your fucking mind?"

"I'm going to, if you don't stop treating me like a 12-year-old," Willow stated, her eyes widening right back. "Give me my phone."

"No phone." Then, before Willow had a chance to react, Lauren grabbed her purse and spun around, heading out of her room.

"What are you *doing*?" Willow cried, so frustrated that she wanted to scream.

"If you're going to persist with this insane, self-destructive behavior, then I *am* going to treat you like a child.

From now on, consider yourself fucking Rapunzel, because you are only leaving this house to go to school and come home, and I will be the one driving you."

"Oh, my *god*." Willow grabbed her head in her hands, her body so hot with anger that she half-expected to combust. "You can't do this!"

"And your counselor," Lauren added. "Twice a week. Once a week is clearly not helping."

Spinning around to appeal to Ashlynn, Willow said, "Are you going to say anything to her?"

Ashlynn shrugged helplessly—but she wasn't helpless, she just wasn't *willing* to help.

Helplessness clawed at her insides. "So, I'm a prisoner in my own goddamn house now, is that it?"

"Willow," Lauren reprimanded, spinning around with her crazy eyes. "Do not use that word."

"I will use whatever *goddamn* word I want to use! Maybe *you* should talk to the counselor about making your daughter, who was held *prisoner,* a *prisoner* in her own home! Way to be helpful, Mom, really. I'm blown away by how much sense that makes."

"I don't care," Lauren stated, shaking her head. "I will not stand by and let some pervert take advantage of my daughter. The fact that he already has makes me sick—your father should've killed the bastard."

Heart sinking, Willow said, "That's a real possibility! I have to call him tomorrow, so I need my phone."

"You can use the house phone. Under supervision."

"Fuck this," Willow yelled, rushing past her mother and down the stairs, aware of their footsteps behind her so she picked up the pace, jerking the door open and not even taking the time to close it behind her.

"Willow!"

Ignoring them, she jogged down the driveway, trying to figure out what the hell she was doing. Without a coat, she couldn't exactly walk in the frigid night air to the hotel, and it wasn't close enough that she would feel safe anyway. While she wasn't as petrified of the night as she had been, she was still afraid, and there was no way she wouldn't fear every car passing by. By the time she made it to the hotel, however many hours later, she would be a wreck.

No, she didn't have to go all the way to Ethan's. She could go to someone's house and use their phone to call Ethan, or even a taxi service. Of course, she had no money. No clothes.

It didn't matter, she didn't need money or clothes. Ethan would have enough to pay the cab, right? He probably wasn't back from Chicago yet—then she realized he was probably on his way *to* Chicago. It would probably be a couple of hours before he got back to the hotel, if he even *went* back to the hotel.

Despair began to catch up with her.

She really was trapped.

Her legs kept moving, she continued running down the road despite the realization, but then she heard a car coming up the road behind her and her insides turned to mush. The sound of Ashlynn calling out the window slowed her heart slightly, but she still felt cornered.

"Please get in the car."

Willow stopped, but didn't get in the car. Instead, she looked Ashlynn in the face, thinking to appeal to her more calmly, more rationally, and said, "I love him."

By the grim look on Ashlynn's face, it had *not* been the right thing to say.

"We care about each other," she continued, since she already started digging the hole. "It isn't sordid like you guys are thinking—I know how it sounds, but it isn't like that. Ethan didn't take advantage of me. He didn't want to hurt me. He was forced as much as I was—we were both forced, they just used him as a tool. You don't get it. He is not a bad person."

"Just get in the car, and we can talk about it," Ashlynn said gingerly.

It was her only hope, so Willow opened the car door and slid inside.

"He's helped me," Willow said immediately. "He helped me with my anger—he's the one who told me go to counseling. Trust me, if Ethan was one of the bad guys, I wouldn't protect him."

"I know you think that," Ashlynn replied, her voice calm. "But I think you need to compromise with us. Surely you can understand… You need to take a step back from him, Willow. He is not your hero, he is not your boyfriend—regardless of how you feel right now, you need to…you need space. No phone and no car for a little while isn't the end of the world."

"I have to call him tomorrow to let him know how the conversation with my dad goes. Ethan's family won't sleep in their house tonight because of what my father did."

"That isn't your problem. We need to focus on taking care of you right now, you can call your father or I will call your father and make sure that he…steers clear. I don't know what happened today, I don't…care, right now what I care about is you."

"Right now what *I* care about is Ethan, and not feeling like a prisoner in my own home. *I'm* fine. I am not some wilting flower, I am not brainwashed, I am not protecting someone who hurts me. Somebody that I care about is going through a rough time right now, and I want to be able to talk to him."

"No," Ashlynn said, somewhere between firm and apologetic. "He's a part of your past, not your future, and honestly…while I don't agree with the way that your mother went about it, I do agree about what needs to happen next. No more Ethan, Willow."

Willow's jaw clenched as Ashlynn turned the car off. "That is my decision to make, Ashlynn."

"Not this time."

"What if I don't listen to you?" she challenged.

"Then we tighten the restrictions even more. Maybe you need to take some time off school, start college a year late."

Her stomach plummeted.

"If we find out you've been trying to talk to him, make no mistake, Willow…we will do whatever we have to do to keep you safe."

Refusing to move, Willow sat in the car while Ashlynn got out, loathing her parents in that moment. Like a bird with clipped wings, all she could think about was escape.

There was no escaping without their cooperation. As difficult as it was, she needed to try to keep her head, try to find a way around their ridiculous restrictions.

But what if she got caught? What if they actually followed through with that threat? It would derail her whole life and she'd be helpless for another year.

Shoving the car door open, she jogged to catch up to Ashlynn, her mind racing. "Wait."

Ashlynn turned to her expectantly.

Taking a breath and then letting it out, Willow said, "Okay, I'll abide by your rules, but I have one request. You have to let me call him one more time to say goodbye."

Her eyes drifted off to the side as she seemed to consider it. Nodding once, she said, "I'll talk to your mom about it."

While Ashlynn went to talk to Lauren, Willow tried to think of a plan. She had kept their relationship a secret before, surely she could manage to see him once in a while, she just needed to figure out how.

If she pretended to roll over and exhibited good behavior for a while, surely she would get her privileges back. She wouldn't call him—they might see that on the phone bill—but if she played them long enough, she would get back her car, and then…assuming he hadn't already moved on or gotten back together with his wife, she could see him again.

Was that really the best case scenario?

Her shoulder drooped at that depressing realization.

Before she had too long to wallow in it, Ashlynn and Lauren came back.

"It's not that we don't trust you," Ashlynn began.

That time, it was Lauren who interrupted. "It is that we don't trust you. You've been lying to us and sneaking around for months. What's more, I think it's best you quit him cold turkey. There will be no contact between you and that piece of shit ever again—not ever. I'm sorry if this makes me the villain in your eyes, but someday you will look back on this and you will understand. You will *thank* me."

"I will *not* thank you," Willow stated.

"We'll see. Either way, this is what's going to happen. I hate to employ that 'as long as you're living under my roof' bullshit, but I'm going to."

"Fine, then I'll move out. I'm 18."

It was a completely empty threat. Without their money or her father's money, she would have to drop out of school to work enough hours to pay for her own place. Still, she had to try.

"Good luck with that," Lauren said, shaking her head tiredly.

The only weapon left at her disposal was a glare, so she turned it up full power. "You're going to regret this," she said, still trying to get Lauren to back down. "I'm only in school for a few more months, then you can't treat me like this anymore."

"We won't have to, because you're a smart girl and eventually you're going to come to your senses. But only with no contact."

Willow shook her head. "This isn't fair. This isn't the way to handle this."

"Maybe not, Willow, but this is *not* something I was prepared for; I have no idea how to handle this."

With that, Lauren turned toward the stairs, but hesitated. "Please go to your room so I don't have to worry that you're trying to run away again."

She debated refusing just to be difficult, but she suddenly felt as exhausted as her mother looked, so she settled with storming wordlessly up the stairs, stomping down the hall, and slamming her bedroom door shut.

# CHAPTER TWENTY FIVE

As he took a sip of the room temperature tea, Ethan made a face, placing it back down and checking the clock on his tablet.

Ten more minutes.

He flicked a glance at the young man behind the counter who sat on a stool, playing with his phone to pass the time.

Turning his gaze to the window, he watched through the glass as absolutely no one walked by or opened the door to come inside.

When Willow didn't call him after she was supposed to talk to her dad, he tried texting her. Calling her. Texting her again.

Part of him wasn't sure if she was mad at him for jumping out of bed *again* right after they'd had sex (he couldn't blame her for being pissed about that), or if it was something else. After checking online, he saw that her accounts hadn't been updated, and it wasn't until hours later, when his message still showed as not being read that he started to worry.

How would he know if something had happened to her? No one would tell him unless they wanted him to try to find her, and after what her father knew, he doubted the man would let that happen again, even if she *was* in danger.

He also didn't need him to. Antonio had his own network of people who could surely handle it.

When two days passed, his messages still unread, he broke down and called her house phone. He hoped she would answer, or even her younger brother, just so he could make sure she was okay.

One of her mothers answered, but the hello was too short for him to know which one.

"Um, hey, is Willow available?"

He grimaced a little—is that what someone calling for Willow would ask?

"Who is this?" she returned sharply.

What did Willow say her scrawny friend's name was? Was it Justin? Maybe he should go with Angel, since he remembered that one. Was he still in the picture?

Before he made a decision, she went on. "Is this Ethan Wilde?"

Well, shit. There was no way that could be good.

And it wasn't. Before he even answered—although his hesitation was probably answer enough—she launched into a tirade, calling him every name in the book, and assuring him she was going to do everything in her power to convince Willow to report what he had done to her so that "his disgusting ass" would rot behind bars.

Someone took the phone from her at the end of the tirade and he held out hope that it might be Willow until he heard a firmer, calmer tone. "Willow no longer has a phone and she isn't allowed to use this one. Don't try to contact her again or we *will* file a restraining order."

It should have occurred to him that the reason Willow's father left without having the final word was that he had another plan. It should have at least crossed his mind, before he let Willow leave that night, that she might be walking into an ambush.

He had been too distracted.

Like he had been distracted, really, since the moment he first laid eyes on the damn girl.

The old Ethan would have thought of all those things. Would have noticed more.

Of course, the old Ethan wouldn't have been involved with her in the first place, so his life wouldn't have been blown to shit and he wouldn't have to worry about angry parents wanting to castrate or kill him.

Oh, how simple life had once been.

Since it didn't seem like Willow was the one who wanted nothing to do with him (there would be no reason to take away her phone if she had agreed to it) he tried to think of some clandestine way to contact her. He knew which school she went to, so even though it made him feel shadier than he was, he lurked in the parking lot one day, hoping he could catch her before she went home.

Her mother picked her up as soon as she walked out of the building, and Willow's head was down, so she didn't see him.

Next, he started going to the Chinese restaurant they had gone to in the evenings and staying there until they closed, hoping she might think of it too, and maybe she would show up.

When they closed, he would go to the basketball court and just park, on the off chance that she would go back there.

It had been six nights, and nothing.

There was no sign of her existence, just like before.

On a whim, a day earlier, he created a fake social media account and tried to friend her, but either it had been ignored, or she hadn't been online since. Surely if she saw it, she would guess it was him.

As he sat in the restaurant, checking the clock again, he found his thoughts drifting back to the prospects he *didn't* enjoy thinking about.

Maybe Willow resisted at first, but in the end, she agreed that cutting him out of her life was a good call. Maybe she was dealing with it like a break-up, and he just hadn't gotten the memo.

Worse: even if she hadn't, maybe it *was* what was best for her. That was almost definitely true. Even if he was in any way right for her at his best, he was so far from his best. His whole life was a mess, he had no idea what was happening with his family, and before the possibility of death had shown up at his door, *he* had been the one wanting to take a step back to protect her. He knew it couldn't end well.

He knew he would hurt her, in the end.

He just hadn't expected the end to come so quickly, and without having a part in the decision.

Wood scraped the cheap tile floor and the guy behind the counter called over to him, "Do you need a box tonight?"

Glancing back at the younger man, Ethan forced a smile and shook his head. "No, not tonight."

One last look at the clock.

One more minute.

Ethan sighed, putting the cover back on his tablet and standing.

He checked his phone, one last time.

It read: 10:30. No more minutes.

Nodding at the man behind the counter, he said, "You have a good night."

The man smiled and nodded back. "Okay, you too. See you tomorrow."

Ethan smiled grimly. "Not this time."

The bell above the door jingled as he pushed it open and stepped out into the frigid night air, and that time, Ethan Wilde headed home.

# About the Author

Sam Mariano has been writing stories since before she could actually write (she just used Barbies back then). She lives in Ohio and has a wonderful daughter and a super supportive, Star Wars-obsessed fiancé.

Her earlier books are Because of You (#1), a coming-of-age story about the power of first love, and Beautiful Mistakes (standalone), a contemporary romance about a Chicago nanny who makes some mistakes, but manages to find her way…maybe! You'll have to read it to find out.

Find Sam on Facebook, Goodreads, or Twitter, though her computer hates Twitter, so she isn't on there too often. She loves to hear from readers!

.

Manufactured by Amazon.ca
Bolton, ON